DUKE ELLINGTON

—— ••• ——

CO

DUKE ELLINGTON

Ron Frankl

Senior Consulting Editor
Nathan Irvin Huggins
Director
W.E.B. Du Bois Institute for Afro-American Research
Harvard University

CHELSEA HOUSE PUBLISHERS
New York   Philadelphia

Editor-in-Chief   Nancy Toff
Executive Editor   Remmel T. Nunn
Managing Editor   Karyn Gullen Browne
Copy Chief   Juliann Barbato
Picture Editor   Adrian G. Allen
Art Director   Giannella Garrett
Manufacturing Manager   Gerald Levine

Staff for DUKE ELLINGTON
Senior Editor   Richard Rennert
Associate Editor   Perry King
Assistant Editor   Gillian Bucky
Copy Editor   Terrance Dolan
Editorial Assistant   Susan DeRosa
Associate Picture Editor   Juliette Dickstein
Picture Researcher   Alan Gottlieb
Senior Designer   Laurie Jewell
Design Assistant   Laura Lang
Production Coordinator   Joseph Romano
Cover Illustration   Alan J. Nahigian

Creative Director   Harold Steinberg

15 14 13 12 11

Library of Congress Cataloging in Publication Data

Frankl, Ron.
   Duke Ellington / Ron Frankl.

   p.   cm.—(Black Americans of achievement)
   Bibliography: p.
   Includes index.
   Summary: Chronicles the life of internationally acclaimed
jazz musician Duke Ellington, from the Harlem Renaissance
through his later years.
   1. Ellington, Duke, 1899–1974—Juvenile literature.
2. Jazz musicians—United States—Biography—Juvenile
literature. [1. Ellington, Duke, 1899–1974. 2. Musicians. 3. Afro-Americans—Biography] I. Title.
II. Series.
ML3930.E44F7   1988   785.42′092′4—dc19 [B]
[92]   87-25396
ISBN 1-55546-584-6
      0-7910-0208-X (pbk.)

CONTENTS

BLACK AMERICANS OF ACHIEVEMENT

Ralph Abernathy
civil rights leader

Muhammad Ali
heavyweight champion

Richard Allen
religious leader and social activist

Louis Armstrong
musician

Arthur Ashe
tennis great

Josephine Baker
entertainer

James Baldwin
author

Benjamin Banneker
scientist and mathematician

Amiri Baraka
poet and playwright

Count Basie
bandleader and composer

Romare Bearden
artist

James Beckwourth
frontiersman

Mary McLeod Bethune
educator

Blanche Bruce
politician

Ralph Bunche
diplomat

George Washington Carver
botanist

Charles Chesnutt
author

Bill Cosby
entertainer

Paul Cuffe
merchant and abolitionist

Father Divine
religious leader

Frederick Douglass
abolitionist editor

Charles Drew
physician

W.E.B. Du Bois
scholar and activist

Paul Laurence Dunbar
poet

Katherine Dunham
dancer and choreographer

Marian Wright Edelman
civil rights leader and lawyer

Duke Ellington
bandleader and composer

Ralph Ellison
author

Julius Erving
basketball great

James Farmer
civil rights leader

Ella Fitzgerald
singer

Marcus Garvey
black-nationalist leader

Dizzy Gillespie
musician

Prince Hall
social reformer

W. C. Handy
father of the blues

William Hastie
educator and politician

Matthew Henson
explorer

Chester Himes
author

Billie Holiday
singer

John Hope
educator

Lena Horne
entertainer

Langston Hughes
poet

Zora Neale Hurston
author

Jesse Jackson
civil rights leader and politician

Jack Johnson
heavyweight champion

James Weldon Johnson
author

Scott Joplin
composer

Barbara Jordan
politician

Martin Luther King, Jr.
civil rights leader

Alain Locke
scholar and educator

Joe Louis
heavyweight champion

Ronald McNair
astronaut

Malcolm X
militant black leader

Thurgood Marshall
Supreme Court justice

Elijah Muhammad
religious leader

Jesse Owens
champion athlete

Charlie Parker
musician

Gordon Parks
photographer

Sidney Poitier
actor

Adam Clayton Powell, Jr.
political leader

Leontyne Price
opera singer

A. Philip Randolph
labor leader

Paul Robeson
singer and actor

Jackie Robinson
baseball great

Bill Russell
basketball great

John Russwurm
publisher

Sojourner Truth
antislavery activist

Harriet Tubman
antislavery activist

Nat Turner
slave revolt leader

Denmark Vesey
slave revolt leader

Madam C. J. Walker
entrepreneur

Booker T. Washington
educator

Harold Washington
politician

Walter White
civil rights leader and author

Richard Wright
author

ON ACHIEVEMENT

Coretta Scott King

Before YOU BEGIN this book, I hope you will ask yourself what the word excellence means to you. I think that it's a question we should all ask, and keep asking as we grow older and change. Because the truest answer to it should never change. When you think of excellence, perhaps you think of success at work; or of becoming wealthy; or meeting the right person, getting married, and having a good family life.

Those important goals are worth striving for, but there is a better way to look at excellence. As Martin Luther King, Jr., said in one of his last sermons, "I want you to be first in love. I want you to be first in moral excellence. I want you to be first in generosity. If you want to be important, wonderful. If you want to be great, wonderful. But recognize that he who is greatest among you shall be your servant."

My husband, Martin Luther King, Jr., knew that the true meaning of achievement is service. When I met him, in 1952, he was already ordained as a Baptist preacher and was working towards a doctoral degree at Boston University. I was studying at the New England Conservatory and dreamed of accomplishments in music. We married a year later, and after I graduated the following year we moved to Montgomery, Alabama. We didn't know it then, but our notions of achievement were about to undergo a dramatic change.

You may have read or heard about what happened next. What began with the boycott of a local bus line grew into a national movement, and by the time he was assassinated in 1968 my husband had fashioned a black movement powerful enough to shatter forever the practice of racial segregation. What you may not have read about is where he got his method for resisting injustice without compromising his religious beliefs.

He got the strategy of nonviolence from a man of a different race, who lived in a distant country, and even practiced a different religion. The man was Mahatma Gandhi, the great leader of India, who devoted his life to serving humanity in the spirit of love and nonviolence. It was in these principles that Martin discovered his method for social reform. More than anything else, those two principles were the key to his achievements.

This book is about black Americans who served society through the excellence of their achievements. It forms a part of the rich history of black men and women in America—a history of stunning accomplishments in every field of human endeavor, from literature and art to science, industry, education, diplomacy, athletics, jurisprudence, even polar exploration.

Not all of the people in this history had the same ideals, but I think you will find something that all of them have in common. Like Martin Luther King, Jr., they all decided to become "drum majors" and serve humanity. In that principle—whether it was expressed in books, inventions, or song—they found something outside themselves to use as a goal and a guide. Something that showed them a way to serve others, instead of living only for themselves.

Reading the stories of these courageous men and women not only helps us discover the principles that we will use to guide our own lives, but it teaches us about our black heritage and about America itself. It is crucial for us to know the heroes and heroines of our history and to realize that the price we paid in our struggle for equality in America was dear. But we must also understand that we have gotten as far as we have partly because America's democratic system and ideals made it possible.

We still are struggling with racism and prejudice. But the great men and women in this series are a tribute to the spirit of our democratic ideals and the system in which they have flourished. And that makes their stories special, and worth knowing. •◖◗•

DUKE
ELLINGTON

1

"STOMP, LOOK,
LISTEN"

O N AN AUTUMN morning in 1927, Duke
Ellington found himself searching frantically for a few
more musicians to play in his band. The 28-year-old
bandleader and composer had been working with only
6 musicians in his group, which was then known as
Duke Ellington and the Washingtonians. However,
the prestigious Cotton Club in New York City, where
his band was scheduled to appear in a noontime audition, required its orchestras to have at least 11
members.

The audition for steady work at the Cotton Club
was the opportunity that Ellington had been seeking
ever since he had arrived in New York four years
earlier. Such an audition was the chance of a lifetime,
and Ellington knew that he could not afford to waste
it: Other groups were also scheduled to arrive sharply
at 12 o'clock to compete for the chance to play regularly at the Harlem nightclub.

Noon came and went, yet Ellington was not able
to find enough musicians to join him at the audition.
If only his manager, Irving Mills, had told him about
the appointment earlier!

By the time Ellington managed to round up 11
men with their instruments and lead them to the
audition, it was well past two o'clock. All he could

*Ellington (holding baton) and his band at the Cotton Club, where
they often played Ellington's own compositions. Some of his song
titles appear as chapter titles in this book.*

Early jazz great Joseph "King" Oliver (holding cornet) was a major influence on trumpeter Louis Armstrong, who played in Oliver's band from 1922 to 1924. Clarinetist Barney Bigard, who joined Ellington's band in 1928, is seated second from right.

do was hope that he and his band would get lucky, and that Harry Block, the manager of the Cotton Club, would agree to hear them despite their lateness.

Ellington knew that even if Block allowed the Washingtonians to audition, it was unlikely that they would get the job. The Cotton Club featured Chicago-style jazz, which was then the most popular type of jazz being played, and had always hired Chicago bands in the past. Although Ellington and his men were now living in New York, most of them were originally from Washington, D.C., which was hardly a center of the latest in jazz styles.

Block had not even wanted to hear Ellington and his band perform, even though Jimmy McHugh, who worked at the Cotton Club as a songwriter, insisted they would be perfect for the club's new show. Block gave in to McHugh and agreed to hear the band only because another group, the Chicago-based Joseph "King" Oliver and His Dixie Syncopators, turned down an offer to play at the club. The new show, which was scheduled to begin later that fall, had already been delayed once. Block was becoming desperate to find a suitable band for the show.

Originally established in 1923, the Cotton Club was one of the most popular nightclubs in New York. Socialites and celebrities gladly made the trip to 142nd Street and Lenox Avenue, where the club was located, to hear hot, exciting jazz and watch wild and original floor shows. Along with the entertainment, the Cotton Club also offered its patrons the opportunity to enjoy alcoholic beverages, which were then illegal under Prohibition laws.

The musicians, singers, dancers, and general staff of the Cotton Club were all black. However, the owner and the manager of the club were white, and they welcomed only white customers. Discrimination of this kind was not unusual even in an area such as Harlem, which had recently become the largest black community in the United States. Relatively few blacks owned large establishments of any kind in 1927, let alone a fancy nightclub.

Yet black entertainers were often popular with white audiences, so the Cotton Club presented the finest black performers in the country and paid them far more than they could hope to earn in smaller clubs and vaudeville theaters. For these entertainers, performing at the Cotton Club fulfilled their ultimate dream. According to bandleader Cab Calloway, "It was a club where you had to be somebody to get in there."

By the time Ellington and the Washingtonians were to audition at the Cotton Club, they had already experienced a good deal more success than most jazz bands. They had been the star attraction at the Kentucky Club, located in New York at 49th Street and Broadway, since 1923. While playing there, the band had developed an original and distinctive sound that

A law enforcement official destroys a barrel of beer during Prohibition. Although it was illegal to manufacture, transport, or sell alcoholic beverages in the United States from 1919 to 1933, millions of Americans continued to drink liquor supplied by organized crime.

Ellington (at the far right, seated by the piano) and the Washingtonians in 1925, during their successful engagement at New York City's Kentucky Club. Saxophonist Otto "Toby" Hardwick stands behind Ellington. Drummer Sonny Greer is at the far left.

had proven to be very popular. The small nightclub was often filled with other musicians interested in hearing the Washingtonians' exciting new music.

Much of the attention that the Washingtonians received was due to Ellington's piano playing, songwriting, and musical arrangements. However, the band's distinctive sound was largely the result of the original trumpet playing of James "Bubber" Miley, a creative soloist who produced a growling sound on his trumpet with the aid of a plunger, or "plumber's helper." By covering and uncovering the bell of his trumpet with the handleless plunger while he was playing, Miley created a whole new vocabulary of musical tones that soon became the trademark of the band's so-called "jungle sound." By 1926, the Washingtonians jungle-style jazz was the talk of the jazz world.

The Washingtonians made live radio broadcasts from the Kentucky Club and were even given the opportunity to make a few records—an honor usually reserved for more established artists. They had developed quite a reputation in a short period of time, but by November 1927 they were ready for the next step up the ladder of success. The Kentucky Club engagement had made them a popular jazz band; the Cotton Club could help them to become stars.

Ellington imagined that by arriving late at their audition, their chance at stardom would have to wait a while longer—one of the competing bands must have already made a big impression on Block and his staff. Yet the Washingtonians were asked to perform soon after they arrived, and once the audition was over, they were offered the job. "The reason for that," Ellington said, "was that the boss, Harry Block, didn't get there till late, either, and didn't hear the others! That's a classic example of being at the right place at the right time with the right thing before the right people."

On December 4, 1927, Duke Ellington and the Washingtonians opened at the Cotton Club. Within weeks, the young bandleader was a sensation, on the road to fulfilling all of his dreams of stardom and acclaim. He would soon accomplish things that no black musician had ever done before. He would play not just in nightclubs but in the greatest concert halls as well. He would travel to the four corners of the earth and meet with presidents and kings, gangsters and poets. He would become one of the most accomplished composers and orchestra leaders in the world, receiving acclaim not only from jazz lovers but from the entire music establishment.

And all of this happened partly because he had shown up two hours late. It is only one example of the charmed life that was Duke Ellington's. ✺

On the menu at the Cotton Club, Harlem's most glamorous night spot, was everything from eggs and steak sandwiches to crabmeat cocktails and Chinese food. The club was also known to serve many different types of alcoholic beverages.

2

"I'M JUST A LUCKY
SO AND SO"

E DWARD KENNEDY ELLINGTON was born on April 29, 1899, in Washington, D.C. For most of his youth, he was an only child; his sister, Ruth, was born when he was 16 years old.

Edward's childhood was unusually happy and carefree for a black American growing up at the turn of the century. His family was very warm and loving, and his boyhood years were remarkably free of problems. When he wrote about his early years much later in his life, he made them sound almost like a fairy tale.

A major factor in Edward's happy childhood was the city in which he grew up. At the time of his birth, there were few places in the United States where it was better for a black to live than in Washington, D.C. In fact, the nation's capital had proven to be something of a haven for black Americans ever since the middle of the 19th century.

Before slavery was abolished by the federal government with the passage of the 13th Amendment in 1865, many free blacks chose to settle in Washington, D.C., because it was the only southern city where they were treated with even a small amount of respect by whites. In the capital city, free blacks

Washington, D.C., the nation's capital and Ellington's hometown, as it looked around 1900. By then, the city had a large and long-established black middle class complete with its own schools, churches, businesses, and clubs.

17

were allowed to hold jobs that had never been offered to them as slaves. Rather than having to labor on farms and plantations, they were able to enjoy careers as barbers, porters, waiters, and houseworkers.

In 1830, there were approximately 6,000 free blacks and 6,000 slaves living in Washington, D.C. By 1860, on the eve of the Civil War, 11,000 free blacks and only 3,000 slaves were living there. The black community in Washington, D.C., continued to grow once the war ended, and blacks soon established their own newspapers, cultural societies, and theater groups in the capital. There was even an active and exciting social scene for elite black families.

Most significantly for Edward, there was a busy and creative music scene. A music professor named J. Henry Lewis created a sensation in the early 1890s when a racially mixed audience attended his staging

A mother and her children enjoy an outing in a Washington, D.C., park. At the turn of the century, much of the city's black population lived in relative comfort and safety—especially when compared with black life-styles in other American cities.

of an oratorio, an operatic presentation based on the Scriptures. In addition to having several musical theaters, the city also had its own black opera company.

Shortly before Edward's birth, the development of a separate black middle and upper class in Washington, D.C., was encouraged by a legal decision that enforced racial segregation. In 1896, the U.S. Supreme Court, the highest court in the country, ruled in the case of *Plessy vs. Ferguson* that segregation of the races was completely legal. The Supreme Court said that it was perfectly acceptable to have separate facilities for blacks and whites, just so long as each facility—a train, a school, a hotel—was judged to be roughly equal in quality.

However, the "separate" part of the Supreme Court's ruling carried far more weight than the "equal." The facilities for blacks were always inferior to those for whites. And to America's great and lasting shame, the "separate but equal" ruling was not overturned by the Supreme Court until more than half a century later.

Excluded by racial prejudice as well as by law from most white facilities, the city's black population proceeded to develop its own social institutions—schools, churches, civic groups, political clubs, music and arts groups—and then made them as good as they could possibly be. Although many of the black residents in the nation's capital did not have as high a standard of living as their white neighbors, they still lived better than most black Americans at that time.

Life for blacks in Washington, D.C., could still be difficult. Prejudice was often evident when blacks came into contact with whites. Also, there were a large number of blacks in the city who were living below the poverty level. However, anyone who was willing to work hard—as Edward's father was—could usually earn a decent living for his family.

Ellington at the age of four. His childhood was an unusually happy one. As he himself admitted, he was spoiled and pampered by his many relatives.

Ellington's sister, Ruth (shown here), was born when her brother was nearly an adult. She spent her teenage years living in Ellington's New York home after his initial success, and the two remained very close throughout his life.

Edward's father, James Edward Ellington, was known to his friends and associates as J.E. By all accounts, he seems to have been a charming man who was fond of music and liked to play the piano. While Edward was growing up, J.E. worked as a butler for a prominent doctor, and he also catered at social functions in wealthy homes around the city. He even worked as a waiter at an affair at the White House. Later in his life, he became a blueprint maker for the U.S. Navy.

The Ellington household was usually loaded with all kinds of good food because of J.E.'s catering connections. Edward's family was not rich by any means, yet they experienced few hardships.

According to Edward, his father apparently enjoyed his modest amount of success:

> J.E. always acted as though he had money, whether he had it or not. He spent and lived like a man who had money, and he raised his family as though he were a millionaire. The best had to be carefully examined to make sure it was good enough for my mother. Maybe he was richer than a millionaire? I'm not sure that he wasn't.

Edward was quick to inherit from his father a sense of style and charm. These qualities would serve him well throughout his life.

Although Edward was in some ways like his father, he was especially close to his mother, Daisy. He maintained that "no one else but my sister Ruth had a mother as great and as beautiful as mine." The daughter of a Washington police captain, she came from a large and very religious family, and she passed on her strong belief in God to both of her children.

Daisy's influence on her son was so great that he talked about her frequently—even late in his life, when she had been dead for many years. He said, "I was pampered and pampered, and spoiled rotten by all the women in the family . . . but my mother never took her eyes off precious little me, her jewel, until

I was four years old." The love and guidance she gave him helped him to develop inner strength and pride in himself. These qualities would also serve him well in the years that lay ahead.

Edward's formal education began at Patterson Elementary School, where he had plenty of friends his own age. Outside of the classroom, he enjoyed such hobbies as painting, drawing, and reading. However, his main interest when he was a youth was baseball. He usually concentrated on playing ball rather than on his homework when the school day was over.

One day, Edward's mother saw him get hit in the head accidentally with a baseball bat. She decided that music might be a safer hobby for "her jewel"

When Ellington was a boy, most of the black children in the United States attended schools that were segregated and inferior to those for white students. However, Washington, D.C., boasted a number of good black schools, including those attended by Ellington.

Ellington was a big fan of the Washington Senators, his hometown's major league baseball team, and once held a job selling refreshments at their games. Walter Johnson, the team's star pitcher who was later elected to baseball's Hall of Fame, is in the bottom row, second from right.

than baseball, so she started Edward on piano lessons with a teacher named Marietta Clinkscales. He had grown up with an appreciation for music from an early age; like his father, his mother often played the piano at home, although she preferred to play religious music. Edward learned the basics of both music and the piano from his music teacher, but he was not a very dedicated student. It seems that he missed almost as many piano lessons as he attended.

By the time Edward was 10 years old, he was still more interested in sports—particularly his first love, baseball—than he was in music. He even got a job selling refreshments in the grandstands for the local major-league baseball team, the Washington Senators. The job enabled him to see his baseball heroes close up while he earned some spending money. The

piano lessons were soon discontinued, and he was never to receive much more in the way of formal musical training.

After attending Garrison Junior High School, Edward was enrolled in Armstrong Technical High School, an all-black vocational school in Washington, D.C. The school's curriculum stressed not only subjects such as arithmetic, algebra, English, and history, but also speech and manners. According to Edward, he was taught that "proper speech and good manners were our first obligations, because as representatives of the Negro race we were to command respect for our people. . . . Negro history was crammed into the curriculum so we would know our people all the way back. They had pride there, the greatest race pride." Partly due to this curriculum, Edward's man-

Ellington's father, James Edward (right), was a poorly educated but industrious man who worked hard to provide a good life for his wife and children. His willingness to spend money as quickly as he could earn it was apparently inherited by his son.

ners and speech soon became flawless, while racial pride became an important part of his personality throughout his life.

Every summer while Edward was growing up, he and his mother took a vacation, usually to the seashore. The summer before he began high school, they went to Asbury Park, New Jersey, for the entire summer season. To keep himself busy, Edward got a job as a dishwasher in a restaurant. While he was working there, he heard about a terrific pianist about his own age named Harvey Brooks. Curious to hear Brooks, he and an older friend stopped in Philadelphia, Pennsylvania, to hear the young piano player on their way home to Washington, D.C.

After hearing Brooks, Edward decided that he, too, wanted to become a musician. He said of Brooks, "He was swinging, and he had a tremendous lefthand, and when I got home I had a real yearning to play. I hadn't been able to get off the ground before, but after hearing him I said to myself, 'man, you're just going to have to do it.' "

Edward never again lost his interest in music. After returning home, he began to spend long hours at practicing the piano, working out sounds that he heard other pianists play. Slowly, he began to master the piano. Although he took a lesson on occasion and asked questions of those who could help him, he basically taught himself how to play. Playing came easily to him; he seemed to have a natural talent for music. He quickly learned how to play popular songs of the day, and he began to write his own tunes as well.

It was at about this time that Edward received the nickname by which he would soon become well known. He became friends with a boy named Edgar McEntree who, despite his young age, was already a fancy dresser and talker with a busy social life. McEntree was very popular and went to a lot of parties. After becoming his friend, Edward began to go to these parties, too. As they moved in elite social circles, McEntree decided that his well-spoken, well-mannered, piano-playing friend needed an elegant nickname to go with his new social status. Edward subsequently became known as "Duke."

Shortly after being nicknamed Duke, the budding musician discovered that music could improve his social life. McEntree announced to everyone at a party that his friend was a talented pianist; Duke was then asked to play. With little choice in the matter, he sat down at the piano and began to play one of his own compositions. The people at the party loved it and called for more.

This was was the first time that Duke was ever cheered for his music, and he loved the feeling of being appreciated. He subsequently played at many parties and became very popular—particularly with the girls, who began to notice his good looks and fancy manners. He said, "I learned that when you were playing the piano there was always a pretty girl standing down at the bass clef end of the piano. I ain't been no athlete since." ☙

Ellington was as deeply devoted to his mother, Daisy Kennedy (shown here), as she was to him. A highly cultured and educated woman, she was also very religious and made a point of passing on her strong faith to both of her children.

"FLAMING YOUTH"

E LLINGTON'S TEENAGE YEARS were as care-free as his childhood. Music continued to play a larger and larger role in his life, but he had other interests as well. In high school, he concentrated on art and drawing, training for a possible career as a commercial artist, and he also held a series of part-time jobs after school.

In 1917, shortly after the United States entered World War I, Ellington got a job with the Navy Department. At first, he worked as a messenger. However, good workers like him were hard to find during wartime, so he was soon given a more responsible job: He became the assistant to a man whose job was to make train reservations for military officers. After Ellington learned his duties, his boss turned over more and more of the office responsibilities to his 18-year-old assistant. It was challenging work, but he enjoyed it.

Around this time, Ellington and his friends, who were still legally underage, would sneak into burlesque theaters, which featured live shows with music, dancing, comedy, and—as Ellington put it—"rather gorgeous girls" dressed in very revealing costumes. Although he admitted having a great interest in

Ellington (center) and Sonny Greer (left) at Louis Thomas's cabaret in Washington, D.C. After several years of playing the piano in Thomas's groups as well as working for him as a solo performer, Ellington decided to go into business for himself and proceeded to organize his own bands.

Oliver "Doc" Perry was a Washington-based pianist who impressed Ellington with his musical ability. The many valuable music lessons that Perry gave to Ellington helped him to pursue his own musical ideas.

watching the beautiful dancers, he also learned a lot about show business and what it took to successfully entertain an audience. These lessons proved to be helpful when he embarked on his own show business career.

Along with going to the burlesque theater, Ellington also liked to spend his free time in pool halls. The main attraction for him was not playing billiards. Instead, he enjoyed the opportunity to listen to the conversations of the older men who also passed the time there. They told stories about their trips to various places around the country, which gave Ellington the urge to travel. He learned about other subjects as well, for the city's black pool halls attracted men from many different professions: gamblers, doctors, athletes, musicians, businessmen, and pickpockets. By listening to their discussions with great interest, Ellington soon developed opinions about politics, sports, and life in general.

However, the greatest attraction that the billiard parlors held for Ellington was the music that he heard there. When many of the best black piano players in Washington, D.C., were not performing elsewhere, they would stop in at the pool halls and play informally. These pianists played a variety of musical styles— mostly ragtime and stride, which were styles, developed by blacks, that were then very popular. Some pianists also played jazz, the exciting, new style of music that was just beginning to gain a large audience.

Ellington spent many hours listening, watching, and learning from these older players. Most of the pianists were very happy to answer his questions, and he was quick to pick up from them their tricks of the trade. He soon began to play the piano in pool halls, developing his own distinctive style by combining many of the musical styles and ideas he heard.

One man in particular played a very large role in advancing Ellington's education on the piano: Oliver "Doc" Perry, a well-schooled musician whose knowledge of music was quite sophisticated. Ellington was very impressed by Perry's piano-playing abilities—as were most people who heard him play—while Perry heard great promise in Ellington's playing. Perry began to tutor the eager young pianist, who gladly absorbed the free musical education that was being offered during these valuable lessons. Ellington said:

> I was invited to his home for refreshments, and one by one he showed me things, some of which I still use. . . . He was my piano parent and nothing was too good for me to try. Even if I didn't learn to play it, I knew how it was done. Doc Perry was probably the first in the parade where I found the right person in the right frame of mind to do all that he could for me and my advancement.

By the time Ellington was 22 years old, he was already a successful pianist and bandleader on Washington, D.C.'s music scene.

Playing a major role in Ellington's musical education, Perry's skill and knowledge enabled the young musician to develop his playing, composing, and arranging abilities. Without the benefit of Perry's lessons, it is possible that only a few people would have heard Ellington's music.

Ellington's musical training was mostly verbal rather than written. Although he mastered some complex musical concepts, he never learned to read written music particularly well. Throughout his career, he relied on his own simple system of notation and memorization. This makes his later accomplishments seem even more impressive, as his natural abilities enabled him to succeed without much formal musical training.

While Ellington was finishing high school, he began to work professionally as a pianist. For a short time, he accompanied a magician. He then began working for a man named Louis Thomas, who owned a cabaret and also provided pianists as well as small musical groups for dances, dinners, and parties. Finding regular work for a number of musicians became for Thomas a very profitable sideline to his nightclub. He negotiated the fee for the music, and the musicians were paid a modest, guaranteed salary from this amount, with Thomas pocketing the difference.

After several years of playing in Thomas's groups and working occasionally as a solo performer, Ellington began to realize that he could probably earn more money on his own. One evening, after his playing had met with great success at a local country club, he collected a fee of $100 for Thomas. It seemed strange to Ellington that his share of this fee should be only $10. Accordingly, he decided to go into business for himself. He placed a few ads in some newspapers and hired musicians to make up a few bands.

Ellington was soon earning a good living by playing at the same type of engagements as when he had been employed by Thomas. Ellington's customers liked his groups. There were some nights when he had four or five different bands playing at various affairs around the city. Before long, he had built up quite a reputation throughout the area.

During this period, Ellington was forced to make a difficult decision. He had shown so much promise as an artist that when he finished high school, he was offered a scholarship to study at the Pratt Institute of Applied Art in New York. It was a wonderful opportunity, especially for someone who enjoyed his art studies. However, Ellington was already becoming a success in the world of music, earning up to $150 a week—an enormous sum in 1918. Besides, music had become his greatest love. With very little regret, he passed up the scholarship. He had decided that his future lay in music.

As a profitable sideline to his growing music career, Ellington started a sign-painting business with a friend. When customers came to order a sign for a dance or a party, Ellington would ask them if they needed music for their affair. If they had not yet hired a band, he would offer the services of his own musicians. For a young man barely out of high school, he was doing very well.

In the summer of 1918, Ellington married Edna Thompson, a childhood friend who came from a good family. She also happened to be a talented pianist. Early in 1919, she gave birth to their son, Mercer.

Ellington's musical career continued to develop in 1919, although his music at that point was not yet jazz. It was a combination of popular dance tunes, ragtime, and stride. However, elements of jazz, which was still in its infancy, were beginning to creep into his playing and songwriting. And although his musical arrangements still reflected the lessons of Perry and others, they also revealed his own emerging, distinctive ideas.

Ellington's wife, Edna Thompson, studied music and played the piano while growing up in Washington, D.C. She supposedly tutored Ellington on the piano and in music theory when they were still in high school.

When James P. Johnson, a New York–based musician and songwriter who was recognized as the master of stride piano, performed at Convention Hall in Washington, D.C., Ellington was listening eagerly in the audience. He had first heard Johnson's music on a piano roll played by a player piano, a mechanical piano that reproduces a pianist's performance that has been recorded on perforated paper rolls. Player pianos were a common source of recorded music in the days before the advent of radios and record players. Ellington was so impressed by Johnson's performance of "Carolina Shout" on the piano roll that he spent days studying and memorizing the movement of the keys on a player piano until he had mastered the song.

During Johnson's live performance, Ellington's friends and fans insisted that as the local favorite, he go up on the stage and "cut" (outplay) the master on his own song. A friendly and gracious man, Johnson let the young musician replace him at the piano. Ellington said of his appearance on stage:

> I was scared stiff, but James P. was not only a master, he was also a great man for encouraging youngsters. He went along with the whole scene, and when I finished "Carolina Shout" he applauded too. I didn't play anymore that night, but just leaned over the piano and listened to the one and only. What I absorbed on that occasion might, I think, have constituted a whole semester in a conservatory. Afterwards, he elected me his guide for a tour of all the Washington joints, and I stayed up until 10 A.M. The friendship that began then was important to me later when we got to New York.

Although Ellington's composing and arranging changed greatly over the course of his career, his piano playing often contained a hint of both the stride style and Johnson's influence. His left hand would alternately play chords and heavy bass notes while

Pianist James P. Johnson, whose stride style was a bridge between ragtime and jazz, composed such hits as "Carolina Shout" and "If I Could Be with You." He was a major influence on both Ellington and Fats Waller, who was once his pupil.

his right hand would play the melody. Stride played an important role in the development of jazz, as the music progressed from its early New Orleans roots to the more urban, northern styles of jazz that became popular in the mid-1920s. Long after stride had all but disappeared from the jazz scene, Ellington's playing provided a reminder of the role it had played in jazz history.

By 1920, Ellington had begun to gather a group of musicians who not only possessed superior musical skills but also had the consistent and dependable per-

Sonny Greer (left) and Ellington (center) with banjo player Sterling Conaway in 1920. The outgoing Greer continued to work with Ellington for more than 30 years.

sonalities that he favored in his musicians. Many popular musicians sometimes took a carefree attitude toward their work. To them, losing a job with one band because of frequent lateness or heavy drinking was not a disaster, for another job was always bound to turn up. However, Ellington was drawn to musicians who were serious about their craft and had made a commitment to their careers that was similar to his own.

In a business where few musicians worked for the same bandleader for more than a couple of years, Ellington's musicians often counted their years of service with him in decades. To reward such loyalty, he kept his groups working as frequently as possible, and they remained on salary whether they were working or not. Along with being well treated by Ellington, his musicians had the opportunity to play his music, which made their jobs more interesting and more challenging than almost any other job they could hope to find.

Two of the mainstays in Ellington's earliest groups were saxophonist Otto "Toby" Hardwick and drummer Sonny Greer. Hardwick was a childhood friend of Ellington's, and his playing had been encouraged by Ellington, who was five years his senior, at an early age. Hardwick joined Ellington's groups when he was old enough to work regularly, and he remained with Ellington—except for a few occasions—until 1946.

Greer, who was originally from Long Branch, New Jersey, first met Ellington while accompanying the great pianist, singer, and songwriter Fats Waller to Washington, D.C., in 1919. The friendly, outgoing drummer soon became close to Ellington. No matter whether he was on stage or was simply with a group of friends, the fun-loving Greer always enjoyed being

Throughout much of his stay with Ellington, drummer Sonny Greer played an impressive percussion arsenal like the one shown here. It closely resembles the entire percussion section of a symphony orchestra rather than the usual jazz drum set.

the center of attention. This became especially apparent after Greer shared in the Washingtonians' Cotton Club success, for he then played one of the largest drum sets ever, with the usual drums and cymbals supplemented by gongs, chimes, tympani, and numerous other percussion devices. A solid if unspectacular drummer, Greer was an occasional vocalist as well, and he remained with Ellington and his bands for more than 30 years.

Ellington and his musicians soon graduated from playing individual engagements to playing more glamorous, long-term gigs in theaters and vaudeville houses. They often worked in an accompanying role for other performers, which was less interesting than playing their own music. However, the work was steady and profitable, and it brought Ellington and his friends into contact with other musicians.

Funny, flamboyant, and extremely talented, Fats Waller achieved fame and fortune as a pianist, songwriter, and vocalist. He composed such well-known songs as "Ain't Misbehavin'," "Honeysuckle Rose," and "The Joint Is Jumpin'."

Through these other musicians, Ellington heard about the exciting music scene that was taking shape in New York City. In particular, there was the area known as Harlem, which was attracting many talented black artists and performers. According to Ellington, "We were awed by the never-ending roll of great talents there, talents in so many fields, in society music and blues, in vaudeville and songwriting, in jazz and theatre, in dancing and comedy. . . . Harlem, to our minds did indeed have the world's most glamorous atmosphere. We had to go there."

Greer was the one who found their ticket to New York. He landed a job there with bandleader Wilbur Sweatman, who featured the gimmick of playing three clarinets at the same time, and then demanded that Sweatman hire Hardwick and Ellington as well. Hardwick went with Greer to New York; Ellington was to join up with them later. However, by the time he arrived in Harlem, work had become scarce for Sweatman's group. Ellington, Hardwick, and Greer were soon splitting hot dogs and scrounging around for whatever work they could find.

Despite the success that the three men had achieved in Washington, D.C., they were just three more new faces in New York. They took advantage of their stay in the city to renew their friendships with James P. Johnson and Fats Waller. Ellington also became friends with Willie "the Lion" Smith, another great master of stride piano, who tutored Ellington on the piano and looked after him whenever possible.

The three Washington musicians absorbed much of the Harlem jazz scene. But with no money, no jobs, and few prospects, New York proved to be a hostile new home. They were back in Washington, D.C., to lick their wounds and rethink their future, as 1922 drew to a close. •〇•

Stride pianist Willie "the Lion" Smith was a colorful character on the Harlem music scene for more than 50 years. When Ellington first arrived in New York, Smith helped him to find performing jobs and tutored him on the piano.

4

"DROP ME OFF IN HARLEM"

————— ❦ —————

THE FIRST BLACK art form to gain popular acceptance with audiences from all different racial and social backgrounds, jazz is a fairly recent development in the world of music. It was born roughly at the turn of the century and has continued to evolve throughout its years of existence. Although the exact meaning of the word *jazz* is unknown, it is believed to have originated in brothels as a slang expression for sex.

The roots of jazz lie in several types of music, including blues, ragtime, spirituals, folk music, and marches. The place where these musical styles were synthesized into jazz was New Orleans, Louisiana, a southern city with a history of mixing nationalities, races, and cultures. Before becoming part of the state of Louisiana, which was established in 1812, New Orleans was ruled at various times by the Spanish, French, and English. Among the people of New Orleans who absorbed the cultural influences of these different nations was a large black slave population, for whom music was a useful escape from the great hardships of life in the city.

Music continued to be an important part of New Orleans culture after slavery was abolished through-

A fashionable couple sporting raccoon coats pose with their flashy roadster in this Harlem street scene. The most stylish era in Harlem's history took place in the 1920s, right at the time of Ellington's arrival in the northern district of New York City.

Gertrude "Ma" Rainey, shown here with her Georgia Jazz Band, was the first blues singer to become nationally known and was among the first to make records. She is often called "the Mother of the Blues."

out the United States in 1865. Blacks and whites began to share in the city's rich musical tradition. Particularly influential in the synthesis of musical styles that took place in New Orleans were the city's many brass bands. Featuring trumpets, trombones, clarinets, snare drums, and a bass drum, these bands were popular attractions at dances, parades, and concerts.

Jazz evolved directly from the music played by black brass bands during the first few years of the 20th century. Musicians such as Buddy Bolden, Freddie Keppard, and King Oliver (all of whom were talented trumpeters) led small groups of five or six pieces that became especially popular with people who liked to dance. The music of these brass bands featured the rhythms of ragtime, the structure of blues, the feeling of spirituals, and the loudness of marching bands. Although every song contained a melody, which was played at both the beginning and the end of the song by the entire group, most of the music was improvised. Instead of being written out and played identically at each performance, this music was spontaneous—always changing and growing—and it was unlike most other types of music that had come before it.

The standard lineup of these earliest jazz groups consisted of one or two trumpets, a trombone, a clarinet, a banjo, a tuba, and drums. However, other instruments, such as a piano, a saxophone, and a bass, were soon introduced into these bands. The trumpet and clarinet were usually the lead instruments. Most or all of the members in the group took solos, with the other musicians playing in support. The songs were mostly instrumentals; even when they were accompanied by lyrics, the singing was secondary to the music.

At a time when dancing was a very popular social activity, the rhythms of early jazz were attractive to a lot of dancers. It was earthy and exciting music, definitely not for polite society. Played mostly in dance halls, honky tonks, and saloons—never in concert halls—jazz was music made for having fun. Proper society condemned it as "the devil's music."

Although jazz was first played by blacks, white musicians soon began to play it as well. Even though their music was often inferior to the music of their black counterparts, most white musicians gained greater financial success while playing jazz than almost all blacks did. Financial success was chiefly dependent upon acceptance by a white audience, and they were quick to favor any accomplishments by whites over similar achievements by blacks.

New Orleans trumpeter and bandleader Freddie Keppard (right) was among the very first musicians to play jazz. He was supposedly offered the opportunity to record as early as 1917 but refused this offer because he did not want other trumpeters to copy his distinctive style.

The first jazz group to make a recording, the Original Dixieland Jazz Band, was a white group that claimed to have invented jazz. Typically, many white listeners chose to believe this falsehood. The practice of white musicians borrowing black musical styles and having greater financial success with them than their creators has continued throughout most of the history of jazz.

Jazz began to spread across America after 1910, when jobs became scarce for musicians in New Orleans. These early jazz pioneers traveled to cities such as Chicago, Illinois, St. Louis, Missouri, and New York in search of work. The audiences in these distant cities liked the new sounds that they were hearing and prompted these musicians to remain away from their base in New Orleans. Chicago soon became the second major outpost for jazz.

The onset of World War I helped to spread the sounds of jazz even more. New Orleans's Storyville district, which housed most of the city's brothels and saloons as well as most of its jazz establishments, was closed down to discourage trouble from occurring among soldiers and sailors, who liked to frequent the area. Not having any place in New Orleans where they could perform, some jazz musicians simply gave up playing music to earn a living. However, others headed north. Chicago absorbed most of these itinerant musicians and became the center of jazz for the next decade. New York became home for some of these New Orleans jazzmen as well.

New Orleans–style jazz remained intact for a few years. Then the sounds of jazz began to change as they became mixed with other types of music, most notably dance orchestra music, which was then very popular. The New Orleans sound lived on throughout the development of jazz by having its most distinctive elements, such as its rhythms and improvised solos, added to dance orchestra music. The resulting style of music was featured by large groups that played

written arrangements. Their music was smoother and more pop-oriented than the original New Orleans style. However, it was unmistakably jazz, and it was soon in demand by the public. In New York, the best of these jazz orchestras was the Fletcher Henderson Orchestra, which eventually featured the greatest New Orleans jazzman of all, trumpeter Louis Armstrong.

The larger number of instruments in these jazz orchestras enabled them to play big ballrooms and nightclubs at a time when there were no microphones or amplifiers. Accordingly, the great volume of these bands made it possible for them to perform for far more people than the old New Orleans combos ever could. The stage was set for jazz to increase in popularity.

The Original Dixieland Jazz (or Jass, as the word was sometimes spelled in jazz's early days) Band, with leader and trumpeter Nick LaRoca (second from right), was apparently the first jazz band to record.

The Fletcher Henderson Orchestra played a major role in the development of jazz. Pianist Henderson is at the far right; saxophonist Don Redman, the first major jazz arranger, is fifth from right; and trumpeter Louis Armstrong, perhaps the greatest of all jazz soloists, stands behind Redman, at center.

It was this new variation of jazz that was rapidly gaining popularity when Ellington and his friends returned to New York City in the spring of 1923. Ellington, Hardwick, and Greer had been playing in Washington, D.C., when their friend Fats Waller told them about a regular gig he was about to quit in New York. When the Washington musicians expressed their interest in the job, Waller even offered to arrange for them to take it over. Hardwick and Greer again went to New York ahead of Ellington, who followed them a few days later. On the train ride north, he spent all of his money on a parlor car and an expensive dinner because he knew there would be a regular job waiting for him when he got to New York.

When Ellington arrived in New York, his friends told him the bad news: Their job had fallen through. As had happened to them the year before, they were stranded, broke, and out of work. Fortunately, they were able to find small jobs through the friends they had made on their last trip to New York. On these jobs, they sat in with a club's regular band and received a share of the tips left by the customers.

While the three friends worked together whenever they could, they continued to search for a steady engagement. They were soon joined by two other musicians from their hometown, trumpeter Arthur Whetsol and banjo player Elmer Snowden, who was several years older than the others. Snowden served as the group's leader until it was discovered that he had been keeping more than his share of the group's money. He was promptly dismissed from the band, and Ellington took over as the leader.

The band was still having trouble finding a steady job when they were assisted by an acquaintance named Ada Smith, who was singing at Barron's Exclusive Club, a popular Harlem night spot owned by a notorious black gangster. Smith, who would soon be-

Ellington and his band landed their first regular engagement in New York at Barron's Exclusive Club, shown here at around 1923. Unlike the Cotton Club, Barron's was a Harlem-based club that catered mostly to black customers.

come a popular singer in Paris under the nickname Bricktop, recommended Ellington and his band for a job at Barron's. The group auditioned at the club and landed the job. "At that time there were no other organized bands in Harlem," Ellington explained.

The pay for the band was low—$30 per week—but the club was popular with entertainers, sports stars, and gangsters who often left generous tips for the musicians. Ellington and his band quickly became a hit with the crowds at Barron's, and on some nights they would share as much as $1,000 in tips. Such a large sum of money was confirmation that Duke Ellington and the Washingtonians, as they were being billed at Barron's, had established themselves on the Harlem scene.

Harlem in the early 1920s was a rapidly growing black community that attracted a large number of intellectual and artistic men and women from all over the United States. One of the few areas in the country where blacks could enjoy an unusually high quality of life, Harlem was, according to clergyman Adam Clayton Powell, Sr., "the symbol of liberty and the Promised Land to Negroes everywhere." A place where its residents could feel good about praising black culture and promoting black values, Harlem in the 1920s became the home of an artistic and intellectual movement known as the Harlem Renaissance.

Music played a significant part in this cultural movement. Talented musicians such as Will Marion Cook, Will Vodery, Fats Waller, Fletcher Henderson, and the songwriting team of Eubie Blake and Noble Sissle added to the growing reputation of Harlem as an artistic center. When Ellington and the Washingtonians landed their gig at Barron's, they were on their way to becoming among the brightest stars on the New York scene.

Ellington happily settled into life in Harlem's black community. He soon brought his wife, Edna, and

their son, Mercer, to live with him in New York, and he maintained a home there for the rest of his life.

Today, record companies control the music industry; but in the 1920s, New York music publishers were the central power in the music business. They bought the rights to the songs that they felt would become hits, often paying as little as $50 per song. Most music publishers made their money through the sale of sheet music. A song became a hit only when thousands of copies of the tune were sold and it was being performed everywhere, by pianists, bands, orchestras, and singers. The song itself became a hit—not a particular artist's version of it.

Noble Sissle (left) and Eubie Blake were two of America's most successful songwriters and performers in the 1920s. Their Broadway musical revue was a major hit with both black and white audiences.

Irving Mills (shown here) was a struggling music publisher until he met Ellington and helped to make him into a star. He served as Ellington's manager and business partner for almost 15 years.

During Ellington's engagement at Barron's, he realized that writing and selling songs could provide a profitable addition to his income. Already a composer for some time, he found a partner named Joe Trent to write lyrics to his music (Ellington used lyricists throughout his career, although he occasionally wrote his own lyrics), and the two joined the large number of songwriters in New York who were trying to sell their songs to music publishers. Ellington and Trent managed to sell a few of their songs, none of which became hits. However, they also wrote a full-length musical revue called *Chocolate Kiddies*, which became a success in 1925. It made promoter and publisher Jack Robbins a wealthy man, although Ellington and Trent did not share in this success because they had sold all of their rights to the show for $500.

These sales marked the beginning of Ellington's career as a professional songwriter. During the next 50 years, he wrote or cowrote more than 2,000 compositions. Learning his lesson from *Chocolate Kiddies*, he retained at least partial ownership of the publishing rights to most of these songs. These rights helped to provide him with a constant source of income for the rest of his life. The money enabled him to keep his band together and on salary even when they were not working regularly. During the early part of Ellington's career, it was unusual for any songwriter to control the copyrights to his own songs. But due largely to his example, it has since become common.

The man who was responsible for helping Ellington to control his publishing rights was a struggling music publisher named Irving Mills. He became friendly with Ellington soon after the Washingtonians moved from Barron's to the Hollywood Club, which was later renamed the Kentucky Club. During the band's four-year stay at the Kentucky Club, Mills became Ellington's manager and booking agent. He also had the wisdom to become an equal partner with Ellington in the publishing of his music. Within a few years, the decision to join forces with Mills would make Ellington rich and would make Mills a wealthy man as well. Their business relationship continued for 15 years.

Although Mills has been accused by some people of taking financial advantage of Ellington by making himself an equal partner in Ellington's affairs, he was also responsible for many of the decisions and developments that made Ellington a star. Mills negotiated the record deals, arranged the Cotton Club audition, and booked safe and successful tours at a time when such travels in America could be difficult for black musicians. He helped to create many of the important opportunities that came Ellington's way early in his career, at a time when such opportunities were usually not available to a black musician.

In return, Mills received a significant percentage of Ellington's income from performances, records, and music publishing. Ellington's musicians were paid from his share of the money, which means that Mills generally made more from Ellington's music than Ellington did. "I owe him a lot," Ellington maintained. "I can't be ungrateful."

Both Ellington and Mills benefited from their relationship in their own way. Mills was the necessary link to the white music industry, and he provided essential guidance in building Ellington's great success. He insisted that Ellington's records feature only his own compositions instead of the works of other people. This ensured larger profits for both men if the songs became hits. Mills also made sure that the band was almost always working, arranging profitable tours and out-of-town engagements in the 1930s, when many bands were struggling to survive due to the Great Depression.

Above all, Mills believed in Ellington's immense talent from the beginning, when it was not at all clear that a black jazz orchestra could become a big success. He worked hard to make Ellington's name

Ellington presents a handsome and elegant image in this 1926 photograph. Although his Cotton Club triumph was more than a year away, he and his band were already the talk of the New York jazz scene.

familiar to both black and white audiences. Ellington later said, "In spite of how much he made on me, I respected the way he had operated. He had always preserved the dignity of my name. Duke Ellington had an unblemished image, and that is the most anybody can do for anybody."

An important change in the Washingtonians' lineup took place in 1925, when Arthur Whetsol returned to Washington, D.C., to study medicine (he later returned to the band for brief periods). His replacement was the talented Bubber Miley, whose trumpet playing further encouraged the Washingtonians' evolution from a dance band into a real jazz group. "Our band changed its character when Bubber came in," Ellington said. The first of many impressive soloists to play with Ellington, Miley also cowrote with Ellington some of the band's greatest songs during his four-year stay with the Washingtonians, including "East St. Louis Toodle-oo," which became Ellington's first theme song.

With their exciting new trumpeter, the Washingtonians' popularity began to grow. Two relatively new inventions—the phonograph and the radio—helped to increase their popularity. These inventions made it possible for new musical styles to be heard in all parts of the country at the same time. Before there were phonograph records and radios, it could take years for a new musical style to spread across the country. Now, for the first time, all of America could enjoy listening to the same entertainers and the same songs.

Just as phonographs and radios were becoming fixtures in every home in the 1920s, jazz happened to be the latest hot musical sound. Accordingly, records and radio brought jazz everywhere at the same time. Although there were other musical styles that had been widely popular before jazz, no previous musical style ever became as instantly popular as jazz did.

Record sales hit a peak in the 1920s that they were not to surpass until 1939. Musicians everywhere were exposed to the new music, and many began to play jazz themselves. Without the advent of records and radios, it is likely that jazz still would have become popular. However, its popularity certainly would not have grown as quickly as it did in the 1920s.

Duke Ellington and the Washingtonians were quick to benefit from both inventions. In 1925, they were given the chance to make live broadcasts of their performances from the Kentucky Club, bringing their playing and Ellington's songs into homes all across the country. They became known nationally without ever having toured outside of the East Coast.

The advent of the phonograph, which enabled recorded performances of the latest hit songs to enter into American homes, played a major role in the spreading of jazz. Early phonographs like the one shown here were powered by a spring that was wound by a handcrank.

In the early days of jazz, records were seldom featured on the radio. Instead, "remote" broadcasts from the nightclubs and ballrooms were presented every night. This practice continued until the 1940s. Many bands and singers built their reputations through these broadcasts, including Ellington's group.

Records first appeared several decades before the radio. The earliest recordings were on wax cylinders, but they were soon put on heavy, fragile shellac disks that look similar to vinyl, long-playing (LP) records. These early records were made on very crude equipment, and they sound terrible by today's standards (the earliest ones were recorded before the invention of electrical microphones). They were played at 78 revolutions per minute instead of 33 1/3 RPM, as is the case with today's LPs. Each disk had one song on each side that was about three minutes long.

The development of the radio almost killed off the popularity of records in the mid-1920s. Music on the radio was free, and the performers often played or sang the most recent hit songs. Most people thought: Why buy a record when music was always available for free on the radio? Record sales dropped steadily after 1925, and then the great economic depression of the 1930s hurt sales even more, forcing most record companies out of business. Fortunately for many musicians' careers, the recording industry survived the competition from radio broadcasts and the effects of a depression.

Mills arranged for the Washingtonians to make their first records in 1925 and 1926. These recordings failed to capture the energy and excitement created by the band in performance, and the songs themselves were not very interesting. By the time the Washingtonians reached the studio again, in 1927, they were better prepared for the challenge of making a first-rate recording.

Bandleader and vocalist Cab Calloway and his band, shown here making a live, remote broadcast for radio, replaced Ellington and his Orchestra at the Cotton Club in 1931.

Trombonist Joe "Tricky Sam" Nanton was an important part of the Ellington sound for almost 20 years. His expressive trombone style, often employing the plunger mute, resulted in sounds that were often compared to the cries of a human voice.

The band's successful engagement at the Kentucky Club continued through 1926 and into the fall of 1927, with Ellington hiring some new musicians who added greatly to the sound of the band. Innovative trombonist Joe "Tricky Sam" Nanton was a distinctive soloist who used the plunger mute to produce music that often resembled the cries of both wild animals and the human voice. Clarinetist Barney Bigard played his instrument in the New Orleans jazz style and was another valuable addition as a soloist.

The most important newcomer to the band was Boston-born Harry Carney. Despite being only 17 years old, he was a master of the deep-voiced baritone saxophone. He was an easygoing and dependable young man who was among Ellington's closest friends in the band. Carney remained a loyal and valued member of Ellington's group for 47 years, until his friend and leader's death.

Even from his early days with the band, Carney traveled to out-of-town jobs and on tours in his own car rather than with the rest of the band. Because Ellington preferred to see the world up close instead of from inside a train or an airplane, he began to ride with Carney, serving as his saxophonist's navigator although never taking the wheel himself. The two men traveled this way for years, often driving straight from one city to the next, barely making it to the following show on time. They would often ride for hours in silence, with Ellington using the time to develop new musical ideas.

By 1926, Ellington and his group were featuring the jungle-style sound that would create such a sensation at the Cotton Club a year later. New compositions by Ellington and Miley stirred additional interest, and many people—including Mills—believed that the Washingtonians were ready to capture a much wider audience. With this in mind, Mills convinced Harry Block to audition Ellington's band in the fall of 1927 for the Cotton Club.

5

"BLACK AND TAN FANTASY"

❦

WHEN ELLINGTON'S BAND began their triumphant engagement at the Cotton Club in 1927, they were advertised as Duke Ellington and His Orchestra. Each evening, the band made nationwide radio broadcasts from the club, and the broadcasts were tremendously successful. The band soon developed a large following around the entire country.

The record companies were quick to notice the band's growing popularity, and Mills, as the band's manager, took full advantage of this eagerness to record the Orchestra's Cotton Club numbers. He arranged for the band to record under a variety of names, such as the Washingtonians, the Jungle Band, the Harlem Feetwarmers, and the Cotton Club Orchestra, as well as Duke Ellington and His Orchestra. This arrangement enabled the band to record the same songs for different record labels without getting sued for violating their recording contracts. The band was so well received at the time that the record companies were more than willing to put up with this situation. Songs such as "Creole Love Call," "The Mooche," and "East St. Louis Toodle-oo"—all songs featured in their Cotton Club performances—were recorded and became hits with record buyers. Above

Ellington and his Orchestra in concert at the London Palladium as part of their triumphant visit to England in 1933. Ellington is at the piano; (from left to right) Freddie Jenkins, Cootie Williams, and Arthur Whetsol are on trumpet, and Joe Nanton, Juan Tizol, and Lawrence Brown are on trombone.

all, the haunting mood of "Black and Tan Fantasy," one of the most effective numbers in their Cotton Club performances, was cited by music critics as evidence that jazz could produce serious, strongly unified compositions and therefore could be more than just popular dance music.

In June 1928, Hardwick left the band (although he was to return a few years later), and Johnny Hodges, a young saxophonist and clarinetist from Boston, Massachusetts, took his place. Hodges quickly established himself as one of the best soloists in the Orchestra, on fast numbers as well as on slow ballads. Over the course of his career, his contribution to the popularity of Duke Ellington and His Orchestra ranked second only to Ellington's.

Hodges's beautiful alto saxophone has become one of the most distinctive sounds in jazz history. Few musicians could improvise a solo on a ballad as impressively as he did. A leading instrumentalist with the band from 1928 until 1951, when he left to pursue a solo career, and from 1955 until his death in 1970, Hodges established the alto sax as a major instrument in jazz. His playing remains one of the most recognizable elements of "the Ellington sound," and Ellington composed many memorable songs over the years that featured Hodges's enormous abilities.

Ellington was only 28 years old when the Cotton Club engagement made him a star and helped him to put all of his financial worries largely behind him. Settled firmly in New York, the city he would call home for the rest of his life, he brought his parents and his sister, Ruth, north from Washington, D.C. They all eventually lived together in a large apartment in Harlem, on Edgecombe Avenue in the fashionable Sugar Hill area.

By that time, Ellington and his wife, Edna, had separated for good. Their marriage had not been a happy one, and they had separated on several oc-

casions before deciding to part permanently after nearly 10 years of marriage. Edna went back to live in Washington, D.C. However, the two were never divorced, and Ellington continued to support Edna in a comfortable manner for the rest of her life.

Because Ellington never discussed Edna or their marriage, very few people who followed his career knew of her existence. Mercer was the only public reminder of their marriage. For a while, he alternated living with both of his parents. He then stayed permanently in New York with his father and the rest of the family.

Saxophonist Otto Hardwick, baritone saxophonist Harry Carney, clarinetist Barney Bigard, and alto saxophonist Johnny Hodges pose (from left to right) in front of an elegant mural at the Cotton Club. Ellington's reed section has always been an important part of the Orchestra's unique sound.

Mildred Dixon (shown here) was a featured dancer at the Cotton Club when Ellington first met her in 1927. She became his constant companion for a decade after he was separated from his wife, Edna.

Ellington did not marry again, but he never lacked female companionship for the rest of his life. He had grown up to be a handsome, charming, successful man who was very popular with women. While he was working at the Cotton Club, Mildred Dixon, an attractive dancer at the club, became his constant companion. Many people assumed her to be his wife, although he was still married to Edna.

As Ellington's public image became well established while he was leading his Orchestra at the Cotton Club, he became the person who was most closely identified with Harlem's glamorous nightlife. He was always well dressed—the picture of elegance and sophistication. His speech was articulate and thoughtful, demonstrating his wit, education, and good upbringing. Above all, he displayed enormous dignity and pride. He was a man of intelligence who appealed to black and white audiences alike.

As the 1930s began, Ellington was a leading example of how much a black man with talent and confidence could achieve in America. He was a positive role model at a time when most blacks were being depicted unfavorably in movies, radio, music, and vaudeville. His tremendous pride kept him from accepting racial discrimination as a reality. He believed that some day blacks would gain equal rights in America and that individual achievements such as his own could help to make that happen.

While Ellington presented a dashing image to the public, he jealously guarded his privacy. He felt the need to keep some distance between himself and the rest of the world. He did this to preserve his own peace of mind and happiness. Throughout his life, he always preferred to devote his time to composing music rather than to socializing.

Ellington lived to compose, to play, and to perform before an appreciative audience. The key to his early success was not his piano playing; although he was more than competent, there were other pianists who played far better. His songwriting was not the key, either; his composing ability had not yet achieved the greatness that he would display later on in his career. His gifts as an orchestral arranger were also still developing.

However, in the early 1930s, Ellington was already demonstrating the ability to produce music that was complex and original yet also very appealing. His music was becoming increasingly different from the music of other leading bands. The "jungle sound" disappeared from his show, and his music moved in a new direction. His songs began to exhibit a willingness to experiment with new or unusual harmonies by blending different musical sounds by different instruments to create a single unified sound. His music started to express moods and emotions that were not often found in jazz or other types of popular music. In doing this, he expanded the basic vocabulary of jazz without sacrificing the energy and excitement that made it popular in the first place. Even as his music grew increasingly sophisticated, he never forgot his first lesson in show business, which he had learned at the burlesque shows: A performer must always remember to entertain his audience.

"Mood Indigo"—a slow, dreamlike melody that became Ellington's first big hit in 1930—exemplified the new direction of his music. *Creole Rhapsody* was his first long composition, filling both sides of a 78 RPM record, which was unusual for a pop record in 1931. It also marked one of the first pieces in jazz history that was complex in form. Both "Mood In-

A performance by singer and actress Ethel Waters (center) is supported by Ellington's Orchestra and the Cotton Club chorus line. One of the most popular black stars in the 1920s and 1930s, she made the first hit recording of the classic song "Stormy Weather."

digo" and *Creole Rhapsody* were evidence of his growth as a composer as well as his ambition to write longer, more serious works.

Perhaps Ellington's greatest accomplishment as a bandleader was his ability to blend the various talents of his musicians. This immense skill was displayed in his recordings of the early 1930s. He brought together the very different styles of his musicians and gave them the opportunity to express their own personalities within the music. No bandleader before or after Ellington has managed this as successfully as he did. Many people have said that his real instrument was not the piano but his Orchestra, a finely crafted group that proved to be ideal for expressing his fresh and personal ideas. By the early 1930s, Ellington's greatest musical triumphs were still to come, yet his many gifts as a musical innovator had already become apparent.

Ellington's musical arrangements often featured his Orchestra's different sections—the saxophones and the clarinets, the trumpets and the trombones—playing passages that were in contrast with each other or that were accompaniments to a soloist. Other groups used these techniques, but Ellington used them in a way that was unique in jazz. His band's musical arrangements often resembled the more complex arrangements of classical orchestras.

By the early 1930s, Duke Ellington and His Orchestra had grown to 13 pieces—including trombonist Lawrence Brown and a new trumpet star, Cootie Williams. A gifted musician, the Alabama-born Williams could play in a style similar to that of the great Louis Armstrong or in the growling manner of Bubber Miley, the man whom he replaced in the band. Ellington also added a young singer to the band: Ivie Anderson, whose warm, expressive voice was featured on Ellington's ballads for more than a decade, including on such hits as "I Got It Bad (And That Ain't Good)."

By 1931, Ellington had grown tired of the routine at the Cotton Club and was ready for some new challenges. Irving Mills began to book the band into theaters in New York and around the country. Ellington proved to be as great an attraction live as he was on radio and on records. He was soon so well known that he was invited to come to the White House by President Herbert Hoover. The following year, he was asked to give a lecture on music at New York University.

Despite receiving these honors, Ellington felt at times that his more sophisticated compositions were being overlooked by audiences in favor of the more commercial-sounding, less creative pop songs that the band also performed. He was eager to gain recognition for his more complex and innovative works, although it seemed as though the American public was not yet ready to accept him as a writer of serious music. Appearances in such short films as *Black and Tan Fantasy*, *Bundle of Blues*, *Belle of the Nineties*, *Murder at the Vanities*, and *Symphony in Black* helped to make the band better known but failed to provide him with the kind of acceptance he was looking to receive.

Ellington's growing sense of frustration at not being taken seriously was eased somewhat in 1933, when Mills arranged for the band to travel to Europe. Their records had been receiving a lot of attention in Europe from both jazz fans and from lovers of classical music. The British in particular were eager to hear Ellington in person, and the Orchestra's performances in England became a major event. "We were amazed by how well informed people were in Britain about us and our records," Ellington said. "The esteem our music was held in was very gratifying." Not only did British royalty come to hear the Orchestra, but the Prince of Wales, who later became the king of England, befriended Ellington and joined the band as a drummer at a party.

The overall tour was a tremendous success. Unlike American audiences, the Europeans sat and listened to the Orchestra with a concentration that was usually reserved for classical music. Ellington was pleased to see that they showed an appreciation for his more ambitious works. "If they think I'm *that* important," he said, "then maybe our music does mean something."

Shortly after Duke Ellington and His Orchestra returned to the United States, they began to tour the country. They remained on the road for most of the next few years. When they toured the South, where travel was usually uncomfortable and often dangerous for black performers because of racism, Mills arranged for the Orchestra to travel in their own private rail-

Ellington onstage at the London Palladium in 1933. His polished manner and stylish wardrobe helped him to become a model of elegance and success—and an important symbol for blacks everywhere.

Barney Bigard (left) and Johnny Hodges pass the time by playing cards—a common activity among musicians on the road. Before air travel was common, bands usually traveled by bus or train, often journeying all day and night to get from one performance to the next.

road cars. This was a much nicer way to travel over long distances than in the crowded buses and cars that were used by most bands. The group ate and slept in the railroad cars, thus avoiding the difficulty of having to find a restaurant or hotel that would accept black patrons.

A musician had to enjoy his life on the road if he wanted to remain a member of the Orchestra, for the band traveled almost constantly. They performed in theaters, ballrooms, and nightclubs around the country, and they made frequent radio broadcasts and records. They even had the chance to make several short films in Hollywood, including *Check and Double Check*, which introduced Ellington's lively, playful tune "Ring Dem Bells."

The band's popularity continued to increase even as America struggled to recover from its great economic depression. Many other large orchestras were forced to break up in the 1930s because few Americans had enough money to spend on luxuries such as music. However, Ellington's unique music made it possible for his Orchestra to thrive even in tough times.

In 1935, Daisy Ellington passed away. Ellington was devastated by his mother's death. He had remained as close to her in his adult life as he had been while he was growing up. For a brief period, he lost all interest in his music. Finally, realizing that he had to do something to regain control of his life, he said to himself: "Now, Edward, you know she would not want you to disintegrate, to collapse into the past,

Duke Ellington and His Orchestra are advertised as the guests of honor at Smalls' Paradise, one of Harlem's most popular nightclubs. By 1935, they were already the country's most popular black jazz band.

WELCOME HOME THE KING OF JAZZ!!

ALLAN McMILLAN INVITES YOU AND YOUR FRIENDS TO ATTEND

SMALLS'

Gala Celeb Party

7th AVENUE AT 135th STREET

Sunday Nite, July 1st

HARLEM'S HOTTEST JAMBOREE WITH AN OUTSTANDING PARADE OF STAGE, SCREEN AND RADIO PERSONALITIES AND SPORTSMEN

GUESTS OF HONOR

DUKE ELLINGTON

And His **FAMOUS ORCHESTRA**

RECEPTION COMMITTEE

Bill Robinson, chairman; Edwin Smalls, Jimmie Ash, Gilbert Holland Bessye Bearden, Romeo Doughtery, Billy Rowe, George Rich, Ted Yates, Al Martin, Jimmie Mordecai, Gene Tyler, Allan McMillan, Frank Gibbs, Joe Jordan, Jimmie Davis Johnny Dancer, Rita Munoz, Bob Williams, Willie Bryant, Teddy Hill Lucky Millinder.

BROADCASTING OVER STATION WNEW 11:45 to 12—3:30 to 4 A. M. Nightly

In 1936, the Cotton Club was moved from its Harlem location to a new site in New York City (shown here), at Broadway and 48th Street, in the heart of the theater district. The club remained a popular attraction for several years before closing for good in 1940.

into your loss, into lengthy negation or destruction. She did not spend all the first part of your life preparing you for this negative attitude."

Ellington began to recover from the depression caused by his mother's death by thinking about the many things he had learned from her. He said, "I believed I could hear the words, her words, and slowly—but never completely—I really did straighten up." He suffered another personal setback two years later, when his father passed away.

Yet Ellington's career as a composer continued to progress through the late 1930s, for his music grew increasingly distinctive and personal. Many of his songs began to reflect an immense pride in his race; his music sought to capture the strength and spirit of black Americans. Among his greatest songs from this period were "In a Sentimental Mood," "Solitude," and "Echoes of Harlem."

In 1936, Mills started his own record company. Ellington was soon recording for him, and he would continue to do so until the two men ended their business relationship three years later. While the Orchestra was recording for Mills, the band also appeared in the film *The Hit Parade of 1937* and played several short, successful engagements in 1938 and 1939 at the Cotton Club, which had moved from Harlem to midtown New York.

For the 1938 Cotton Club appearances, Ellington coauthored an entire show of new music which was called "The Cotton Club Revue." The show featured "I Let a Song Go Out of My Heart," which became a big hit. He was profiled in an article in *Life*, one of the country's leading magazines, that same year.

Also in 1938, a new woman entered Ellington's life. Beatrice Ellis, nicknamed Evie, was a showgirl at the Cotton Club when Ellington first met her. His relationship with Mildred Dixon ended shortly after this meeting. He lived with Evie Ellington (as she

Ellington and his companion Beatrice Ellis (right), who was also known by the nickname of Evie, relax at a nightclub. Their relationship began in 1938, and they remained together for the rest of his life.

liked to call herself even though she and Ellington were never married) for the rest of his life.

Ellington again brought his band to Europe in March 1939, just as Adolf Hitler's Nazi party in Germany was preparing to plunge the entire continent into war. Jazz had become even more popular in Europe than when the band had toured there six years before. Their trip was a great success as the band visited Sweden, Belgium, France, Holland, and Denmark, playing before enthusiastic crowds everywhere they went. When Ellington turned 40 years old, countless fans in Sweden sent him flowers to help celebrate the event.

The Orchestra returned to the United States only months before the outbreak of World War II in Europe. Ellington's popularity was at an all-time high, and he was producing some of the best music he had ever created. Yet his efforts did not stop there. Quite soon, he was to begin an even greater period in his career. ◖◗

6

"JUMP FOR JOY"

——— ❦ ———

A NEW JAZZ STYLE has been developed in virtually every decade of jazz history. Usually, this new style has gone on to replace the kind of jazz that was then currently popular. In the 1920s, orchestral jazz replaced the New Orleans style. In the 1930s, a change occurred once again. Swing, which had its origins in the Fletcher Henderson Orchestra in the late 1920s, became the new sound of jazz in the mid-1930s. At no time in the history of jazz has a particular style been so widely accepted by the public as swing.

The rhythms of swing were very different from the rhythms of the jazz styles that had preceded it. The main reason for this difference is because swing was created especially for dancing. Not only was every beat in swing accented equally, but the rhythms in most pieces of swing remained consistent throughout the song. Unlike jazz of the 1920s, including Ellington's early music, swing was light and fast. As the term *swing* suggests, the music "swung." It all but invited the listener to get up and dance.

Swing was usually played by groups with 10 to 15 musicians. These groups played written arrangements that featured occasional instrumental solos. The key to a swing band was its rhythm section—the piano, guitar, bass, and drums—which worked together to produce the groundwork for good dance music. An accomplished rhythm section could propel the music

Ellington clowns around with chorus girl Louise Franklin in a publicity photo for Jump for Joy. *He wrote most of the music for this 1941 musical revue, which offered a groundbreaking look at contemporary black life.*

The rhythm section had a more prominent role in swing than in earlier jazz styles. By the mid-1930s, Ellington occasionally used two bassists on his rhythm team to provide a more powerful and complex foundation for the music. Shown here (clockwise from top) are guitarist Fred Guy, bassist Billy Taylor, drummer Sonny Greer, and bassist Hayes Alvis.

forward with the same dependability that is found in a well-oiled machine. The bass player usually had the responsibility of keeping the beat, freeing the drummer to accent and complement the music. This new role for the drummer was the most noticeable feature of swing.

New York–based groups such as the Fletcher Henderson Orchestra and McKinney's Cotton Pickers were among the first bands to play swing. However, it was musicians and bands from the Midwest and Southwest who made the new style popular. Kansas City, Missouri, in particular produced a large number of swing greats. The Bennie Moten Orchestra was one of the first and best of the Kansas City bands. After Moten's death, the group's pianist, William "Count" Basie started a band using many of the same musicians. Basie's music was simple yet very wild and exciting. The band featured such outstanding musicians as trumpeter Buck Clayton, drummer Jo Jones, and Lester Young on tenor sax. Basie built his reputation

The Bennie Moten Orchestra (shown here) was among the top Kansas City swing bands. Many of the band's musicians joined the orchestra of Count Basie (seated at the left piano) after Moten (seated at the right piano) died in 1935.

Tenor saxophonist Ben Webster (shown here) was the first great tenor soloist in Ellington's Orchestra. Strongly influenced on his instrument by the great Coleman Hawkins, he joined Ellington for an eventful three years beginning in 1940.

largely through radio and records, and by 1938 his popularity rivaled Ellington's among black swing bands.

When white musicians heard swing, they began to play it, too. As had happened with New Orleans–style jazz, white swing groups soon surpassed black groups in both popularity and financial success. Orchestras led by Benny Goodman and Artie Shaw were among the most popular white swing bands, as white audiences chose once again to listen to white imitations of black music.

Goodman sought to overcome such racial separatism by integrating his band. Accordingly, he became the first white bandleader to feature black musicians in his group. They were usually star soloists who later became successful bandleaders on their own. Goodman also hired Fletcher Henderson, who could no longer afford to keep his own orchestra together, to write musical arrangements for the band. By breaking down some of the barriers that existed between blacks and whites in the jazz world, Goodman prompted many of his white fans to listen to the music of black bandleaders such as Basie and Ellington.

As swing music began to take hold, Ellington's music started to undergo some changes as well. Although his orchestra never really became a swing band, it began to include many elements of the new style. Ellington's music had clearly been moving in that direction since the early 1930s, and the addition of several key musicians in 1939 and 1940 pushed his band's music ever closer to swing.

Powerful tenor saxophonist Ben Webster became an important instrumental voice in what would turn out to be Ellington's finest era. Webster, who came from the Kansas City jazz tradition, had played with many well-known bands—including brief stints with Ellington's Orchestra in 1935 and 1936—before joining Ellington's lineup full-time in 1940. An impor-

tant and original player on the tenor sax, he was featured by Ellington on such classics as "Cotton Tail" and "All Too Soon."

Jimmy Blanton, who also joined the Orchestra in 1939, is now regarded as the most influential bassist ever to play the instrument in jazz. Virtually every popular bassist who has played since the well-schooled Blanton has in some way reflected his revolutionary approach to the bass. He was an outstanding soloist on an instrument that had previously been played only to keep the beat. By introducing the bass as a solo voice, he gave bass playing a freedom that no other bassist had ever enjoyed before. He also had innovative ideas about rhythm and harmony that influenced not only other bassists and other instrumentalists but also arrangers such as Ellington.

The first white bandleader to hire and feature black musicians, clarinetist Benny Goodman (center) led the most popular band of the swing era. His orchestra is shown here playing in 1937 for an integrated audience, which was a rarity in many places at that time.

Ellington in a characteristic pose: working on new musical scores for his Orchestra. More than just a career, music often seemed to be the only thing that mattered deeply to him. He maintained, "Music is my mistress, and she plays second fiddle to no one."

The third major addition to Duke Ellington and His Orchestra during the swing era was Billy Strayhorn, a quiet young man from Pittsburgh, Pennsylvania. Born in 1915, Strayhorn was formally educated in classical music, which remained his chief musical interest until he heard Ellington's music in 1934. Shortly after Ellington and Strayhorn met in December 1938, they became close friends. Before long, they were collaborating on musical ideas—and would continue to do so for almost 30 years.

When the two men composed music together, Ellington often used his friend's talents to develop and shape his own musical ideas. Strayhorn's impressive musical knowledge became an important influence on Ellington, who was inspired by Strayhorn's contributions to compose more complex and ambitious works. Strayhorn was the only regular musical collaborator that Ellington ever had.

Strayhorn also wrote memorable, sophisticated songs on his own that would quickly become an important part of the Ellington sound. These songs included such numbers as "Lush Life," "Chelsea Bridge," and "Take the A Train," which became the band's theme song. He also wrote many arrangements for Ellington, and his orchestrations for the band are among the group's most interesting pieces.

For Ellington, the years from 1940 to 1943 marked his most productive and successful period. Just as the decade began, he signed a contract with the Victor Recording Company, which at that time was the world's largest and most prestigious record company. He recorded often with Victor and was granted the freedom to explore new musical ideas and directions. Such songs as "Sophisticated Lady," "Ko Ko," "Harlem Air Shaft," and "I Got It Bad (And That Ain't Good)" quickly became classics. Full of ambition and energy, Ellington continued to broadcast every night, and he saw his efforts rewarded with great success. In 1940, he took in more than a million dollars before expenses.

Composer, arranger, and pianist Billy Strayhorn (shown here) worked with Ellington for 28 years, assisting him with his composing and arranging while also writing and arranging some of the Orchestra's most important performances.

The band toured the country continuously, playing to enthusiastic dancers and listeners wherever they went. The crowds sometimes consisted of both blacks and whites. However, many theaters and ballrooms would not allow black and white patrons to mix. In some places, separate sections were set up exclusively for the use of blacks, whereas other places excluded them completely.

Duke Ellington and His Orchestra suffered a setback in 1940, when Cootie Williams left the band to join Benny Goodman's orchestra. Shortly before Williams departed, Ellington wrote "Concerto for Cootie," a song that emphasized the trumpeter's enormous talents. Of all the pieces that Ellington wrote to feature a particular musician's skills, "Concerto for Cootie" is among his greatest. Although the music is obviously jazz, the song also fits the traditional definition of a concerto, which features an instrumental soloist accompanied by an orchestra and has

An enthusiastic couple does the jitterbug, an energetic dance that was very popular during the swing era.

three or more contrasting musical sections. "Concerto for Cootie" possesses a beauty and sophistication very similar to a fine classical work.

Williams was replaced on trumpet by Ray Nance, whose very different style of playing the trumpet was soon featured on "Take the A Train." Containing a simple yet engaging melody, it was one of the first pieces to be issued by Ellington when he established his own music publishing company, Tempo Music.

In the summer of 1941, Ellington wrote the music for the show *Jump for Joy*, a musical celebration of black life in America. Presented for three months in Hollywood, the show predicted a brighter future for all black Americans. Ellington and the band were featured in the show along with vocalists Ivie Anderson, Herb Jeffries, and Dorothy Dandridge, who was one of the most exciting new talents in the world of black entertainment.

The original idea for *Jump for Joy* came from a group in Hollywood who saw the show as a way to promote the cause of civil rights for blacks. Ellington was only too glad to participate. *Jump for Joy* was one of his first—and few—direct contributions to the cause of civil rights. Although the show was not a financial success, it received much praise.

At the end of 1941, the lives of most Americans began to change as the United States entered World War II. One of these changes involved travel restrictions for civilians in order to conserve supplies for the war effort. Yet Ellington and the band were permitted to travel all over the country to play for servicemen and civilians alike. The band was also featured in a series of broadcasts put on by the U.S. Treasury Department to sell war bonds.

During the war years, a strike by the musicians' union made it impossible for Ellington or any other performer to record. More than two years of the Orchestra's work went unrecorded, although the group

Ellington and singer Joya Sherrill (standing at center) perform for an audience of servicemen in 1942. Ellington and his Orchestra often entertained military personnel throughout the United States during World War II.

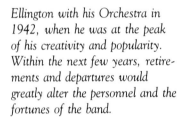

Ellington with his Orchestra in 1942, when he was at the peak of his creativity and popularity. Within the next few years, retirements and departures would greatly alter the personnel and the fortunes of the band.

remained active throughout the period. One of their major activities was playing at the Hurricane Club in New York. "We were at the Hurricane in 1943 for six months and lost money," Ellington said. "But we were on the air five or six times a week and, when we went back on the road, we could charge five to ten times as much as we could before that."

In between the tours, Duke Ellington and His Orchestra gave a concert on January 23, 1943, at New York's Carnegie Hall, then the most prestigious concert hall in America for classical music. Benny Goodman had presented jazz at Carnegie Hall in the past, but no black jazz group had ever been featured there before Ellington. He realized that playing at Carnegie Hall was a tremendous opportunity for him to have his music taken seriously.

Ellington had been interested in writing long pieces of music for some time. With the Carnegie Hall con-

cert in mind, he began work on his first full-length composition, *Black, Brown, and Beige*. It was an ambitious work that attempted to use music to depict all of the major elements of black life in America, including religion, work, patriotism, and civil rights. Although the composition was still rooted in jazz, *Black, Brown, and Beige* represented the direction in which Ellington was looking to take his music in the future.

The portion of the Carnegie Hall concert during which the band played *Black, Brown, and Beige* left the audience a little bit confused. The composition was very different from Ellington's previous music both in length and in style. Many of the listeners felt that some of his greatest strengths as a composer, such as his beautiful melodies and his striking arrangements, were hidden in this longer work. The *Herald Tribune* called it "formless and meaningless—

A revolutionary bassist, Jimmy Blanton (shown here) forever changed the role of his instrument in jazz. He joined Ellington's Orchestra in 1939, when he was only 18, and spent two years with the band before he died from tuberculosis in 1942.

nothing emerged but a gaudy potpourri of tutti dance passages and solo virtuoso work." Ellington was hurt by such criticism because he felt that the nearly one-hour-long composition was his greatest accomplishment to date.

In December 1943, Ellington gave another concert at Carnegie Hall. For that evening's program, he promised to play only shorter, more familiar works. Although he would soon return to composing longer pieces, for which he used the classical term *suite*, he had been deeply disappointed by the reaction to *Black, Brown, and Beige*. He recorded a pared-down, 18-minute version of the piece in December 1944 and did not return to it in a recording studio for almost 15 years. By then, the form of the composition had become quite different from the original version.

Despite the critical reactions to *Black, Brown, and Beige*, Ellington's Carnegie Hall concerts proved to be a huge commercial success. The performances forever changed the way that the public viewed Ellington and his great orchestra. The band was separated from the ranks of other jazz and pop bands and was hailed as a creator of some of the most original sounds in the entire world of music. They were a group of musicians ideally suited for presenting their leader's ideas. Accordingly, Ellington was regarded as an exceptional bandleader as well as an important and unique composer.

The Carnegie Hall concerts of 1943 started a musical tradition for Ellington. He and his band would return to the prestigious hall every year until the early 1950s. Their annual concerts were extremely popular and were regarded as major events in the music world. Always anxious to build his reputation as a serious composer, Ellington used these concerts to premiere a new suite each year.

For various reasons, some of the musicians left the band during the war years. Bassist Jimmy Blanton took leave of the band when he became ill with

tuberculosis; he died shortly thereafter. Ben Webster left to pursue a solo career. Other veterans, such as Otto Hardwick, Barney Bigard, and vocalist Ivie Anderson, tired of the endless travel and chose to settle in one place. They were replaced by talented newcomers such as clarinetist/saxophonists Jimmy Hamilton and Russell Procope and trumpeter Cat Anderson. Old hands such as Harry Carney, Johnny Hodges, and Sonny Greer remained the backbone of the band.

According to the yearly readers' poll in *Down Beat* magazine, Duke Ellington and His Orchestra was the leading jazz band in the country from 1942 through 1946. Despite his band's celebrated status, Ellington was far more interested in being appreciated for his music than in being popular. Yet the changes in the band's personnel would soon affect the Orchestra's preeminent status in the jazz world, and this would result in some challenging times in the years that lay ahead. ❧

Saxophonist Ben Webster (center) and clarinetist Jimmy Hamilton (right) join Ellington during a rehearsal for a concert at New York's prestigious Carnegie Hall. The Orchestra's annual performances at the concert hall began in 1943 and were a major musical event for a decade.

7

"RIDIN' ON A
BLUE NOTE"

❧

SEVERAL YOUNG JAZZ musicians—including trumpeter Dizzy Gillespie, pianist Thelonious Monk, and saxophonist Charlie Parker—met in New York in the early 1940s and began to play a radical, new type of jazz that came to be known as bebop. A complex and progressive music that challenged musicians and audiences alike, bebop was definitely not made for dancing. Although it was exciting music, featuring eccentric rhythms and abrupt accents, its unusual sounds made it difficult for bebop to become as popular as swing.

In the late 1940s, many jazz fans who had been following swing began to listen to other types of music rather than to bebop. For the first time in more than a decade, jazz ceased to be the most popular type of music in America. Accordingly, this meant changes in the economics of jazz. The big bands of the swing era were no longer able to fill up theaters and ballrooms. They had to play in small nightclubs where they were unable to earn much money, use fewer musicians, or get out of the music business entirely.

Ellington was one of the few orchestra leaders who managed to keep his band together during the late 1940s and early 1950s. However, it was not an easy thing for him to do. There was no way for him to be sure that he would make money on long tours. Consequently, he often had to play extended nightclub

Ellington takes a break backstage during a nightclub engagement in 1948. His dressing room was equipped with a piano, which enabled him to work on new music between sets.

Alto saxophonist Charlie Parker (shown here) was one of the originators of the bebop style that gained prominence in the 1940s. His innovative approach to harmony and rhythm resulted in his becoming the most important jazz soloist since Louis Armstrong.

engagements in New York and other cities to keep the money coming in so he could pay his band.

Although Ellington grew discouraged by the band's decreasing popularity, he felt as though he had little choice but to keep the group intact. He said, "It's a matter of whether you want to play music or make money, I guess. I like to keep a band so that I can write and hear the music the next day. The only way to do that is to pay the band and keep it on tap fifty-two weeks a year."

Without his Orchestra, Ellington could not have his music played exactly as he intended it. He maintained, "If it were not for my band, how could I hear my music?" So he kept his band going even when it caused him to lose money.

Many critics who saw Ellington's Orchestra in the early 1950s felt that the music was uninspired, which had never been their impression during the band's previous years. The musicians, including their leader, seemed bored and discouraged. Ellington was writing fewer songs, and many of his compositions seemed to be inferior to his work of the early 1940s. For the first time since he took piano lessons with Marietta Clinkscales, Ellington seemed to be losing interest in music.

The crushing blow to the Orchestra came in 1951. Johnny Hodges, Lawrence Brown, and Sonny Greer left the band at the same time. Hodges and Brown had been important soloists since the band's Cotton Club days. Greer had been Ellington's drummer and friend for more than 30 years, since their early days together in Washington, D.C. Although each of the three musicians felt that it was time for a change and that they could do better on their own or in other bands, their departure hurt Ellington very deeply. Characteristically, he did not give up his desire to lead an orchestra. He soon recruited talented young musicians such as tenor saxophonist Paul Gonsalves and trumpeter Clark Terry, both of whom had worked with Count Basie, to join the band.

This new lineup recorded often in the early 1950s. However, many of the songs that they recorded were simply new versions of earlier successes and did little to add to the band's reputation. They also toured the country steadily and returned to play in Europe several times. Yet the band's performances were inconsistent and Ellington's own enthusiasm was often lacking. British audiences in particular noticed how uninspired the Orchestra sounded and appeared on their 1951 tour. Longtime fans and music critics alike decided that perhaps Ellington's greatest achievements had already taken place.

An indication of how badly things were going for the band came in the summer of 1955, when Ellington accepted a lengthy engagement as the accompanying band for a swimming show called "Aquacades" held in a park on the edge of New York City. For this show, he used only two-thirds of the band and played little interesting music. With no well-paying jobs coming the band's way, it seemed as though the final days of Duke Ellington and His Orchestra were at hand.

Not even Ellington himself could have predicted the events of the following year. By the summer of 1956, he was once again the sensation of the jazz world, on the way to achieving greater triumphs than he had ever known. ◑

Alto saxophonist Johnny Hodges (right) was Ellington's most distinctive and popular soloist for 23 years. His sudden departure from the Orchestra in 1951 shocked the jazz world, but he returned to the band 4 years later and stayed for another 15 years.

8

"SUCH SWEET THUNDER"

─────── ⚜ ───────

BY THE BEGINNING of 1956, the musicians who had joined the Ellington Orchestra in the early 1950s had been with the band for a few years. Each of them brought to the group a personal style that was very different from the styles of the older musicians whom they had replaced. Paul Gonsalves and Clark Terry in particular belonged to a younger generation than Ellington and his original band and had absorbed the most recent developments in the jazz world.

Ellington recognized the talents of his current band members and—as he had done two decades before—began to compose music with their strengths in mind. As he did so, his interest in music increased and his work displayed an originality and energy that had often been missing in the years since World War II. His piano playing, which had often been hidden behind the other strengths of the band, was featured more and more. Although he may not have been a great pianist, his style was very personal and distinctive.

The overall ability of the soloists in the 1956 Ellington Orchestra was probably even greater than those in the classic band of the early 1940s. Terry's trumpet and Gonsalves's tenor sax were the most inspired solo voices. Sam Woodyard was a strong, swinging drummer whose playing was more subtle and

Ellington takes a break in the studio during a 1961 recording session for the soundtrack of the film Paris Blues. *He also composed the musical score for two other movies,* Anatomy of a Murder *and* Assault on a Queen.

flexible than Sonny Greer's. Trombonist Britt Wood-man was another important soloist, and veterans Ray Nance and Cat Anderson on trumpet and Russell Procope and Jimmy Hamilton on saxophone remained important parts of the Ellington sound. Baritone sax player Harry Carney, who had been with the Orchestra since 1927, was still a major soloist. Another significant band member was alto saxophonist Johnny Hodges, who had returned to the group in 1955, having discovered how difficult it could be to lead a band on his own. Although many jazz listeners seemed to have forgotten about Duke Ellington and His Orchestra, all of the pieces were in place for a comeback.

The opportunity for a comeback came in early 1956, shortly after Ellington and the band made some recordings for a small company. The recordings consisted mostly of older songs that had been rearranged to feature the abilities of the band's current musicians. Although the album did not turn out to be a big seller, it received good reviews and attracted new interest in Ellington. Columbia Records, by then the biggest and most important record company in the country, offered Ellington a contract to record for them. The company would allow him to develop whatever projects he chose, including full-length compositions. Recording for powerful Columbia was certainly the best way for Ellington to reestablish his Orchestra as a major force in the music world.

The next big break for the band came on July 7, 1956, when Ellington and his Orchestra were invited to perform at the Newport Jazz Festival in Newport, Rhode Island. A celebration of jazz that stretched over a period of several days, the festival presented the leading jazz stars from both the present and the past to a largely middle-class audience. Ellington and the band were the closing act of the festival, and delays in the day's program made it impossible for them to take the stage until 15 minutes before mid-

night. By that time, much of the large crowd was already heading for the exits after sitting through a long weekend of music.

Ellington opened his portion of the program with a new, longer work entitled *The Newport Jazz Festival Suite*. The remaining crowd liked what they heard and decided to stay for the rest of the program.

Next came a new version of "Diminuendo and Crescendo in Blue," a piece from the late 1930s. In its new form, the music sounded terrific. The striking originality of Ellington's arrangement was fascinating to an audience raised on modern jazz. In the middle of the number, Paul Gonsalves, playing the tenor sax, took a long, exciting solo that continued for chorus after chorus after chorus. The people in the crowd began to go wild, clapping and rising to their feet, screaming with excitement and enthusiasm over

Tenor saxophonist Paul Gonsalves (left) steps to the microphone for a solo—the kind that electrified the crowd during the Orchestra's performance at the Newport Jazz Festival in 1956. Only baritone sax player Harry Carney had more years of continuous service with the band than Gonsalves.

One month after the band's exciting performance at the Newport Jazz Festival in 1956, Ellington was featured on the cover of Time *magazine. Such exposure helped him to win back old fans and make new ones.*

the music. A reviewer for *Down Beat* said that the scene "was transformed as if struck by a thunderbolt . . . the whole band, inspired by the reaction they had started, put their all into the work."

Gonsalves played on and on for 27 choruses, offering one new musical idea after another. When he finally ended his solo, the excitement could not have been any greater. George Wein, the promoter of the festival, was worried that the audience would begin to riot.

"Diminuendo and Crescendo in Blue" continued to its impressive conclusion and was followed by four other musical numbers. The rest of the performance was also greeted with wild applause, leaving no doubt that Duke Ellington and His Orchestra was the hit of the festival. Fortunately for all concerned, Columbia Records captured the historic event on record so that it can still be enjoyed today.

After Ellington's triumphant concert at the Newport Jazz Festival, he was once again on top of the jazz world. His picture appeared a month later on the cover of *Time* magazine, accompanied by a story that said the concert "confirmed a turning point in a career." Accordingly, the next few years proved to be busy ones, and music fans around the world followed his activities very closely.

During this period, Ellington concentrated mostly on writing longer works—including *A Drum Is a Woman*, which traces the history of jazz, and *Such Sweet Thunder*, which is based on characters from the plays of William Shakespeare—producing more than 30 long concert pieces in all. He also wrote the music for a film called *Anatomy of a Murder* and continued to record frequently. The band returned to the Newport Jazz Festival each year and played other jazz festivals as well. In both 1958 and 1959, they went on highly successful tours of Europe. Ellington, at the age of 60, had finally achieved the status that he had sought for so long.

Ellington's great surge of creativity continued without interruption into the 1960s. Both short and long compositions flowed from his pen and were played on his piano. As always, these compositions were written with the assistance of Billy Strayhorn. "Any time I was in the throes of debate with myself," Ellington maintained, "we would talk, and then the world would come into focus."

Ellington also made several fascinating records with some of the stars of the modern jazz scene. They were usually musicians who were a generation younger than he was. Chief among them was John Coltrane, a uniquely talented tenor saxophonist whose influential recordings featured his progressive, passionate playing. His music was as different from Ellington's as almost anyone else's in jazz. Yet Ellington and Coltrane found a musical meeting place, and their record, *Duke Ellington and John Coltrane*, brought out some of the best musicianship in both men. Often neglected and unappreciated, Ellington's piano play-

Ellington meets with Queen Elizabeth II at the Leeds Music Festival during his band's triumphant return to England in 1958. Her Majesty was just one of many world-renowned figures with whom he became acquainted during his long career.

Ellington speaks with a musician in India during an international tour in 1963 that was sponsored by the U.S. State Department. Traveling all over the world in the 1960s and 1970s, his Orchestra encountered enthusiastic audiences everywhere it went.

ing was featured more frequently in the 1960s, and he gained new respect from the jazz world for his instrumental skills.

At the request of the U.S. State Department, the branch of the federal government that is responsible for America's relations with other countries, Duke Ellington and His Orchestra traveled to the Middle East, Africa, and the Far East in 1963. They performed for audiences that had seldom, if ever, heard jazz or any other American music, and they won new fans everywhere they played. The band's own tours of Europe and Japan followed, and they spent much of the year on the road.

Although the overseas tours were very long and exhausting, they were a tremendous thrill for Ellington, who still loved to travel and experience new things. These international tours became a welcome part of each year's schedule for the rest of Ellington's life. They were a huge success and were clearly one of the highlights of his musical career.

In 1964, Ellington's son, Mercer, at the age of 45, joined the band. Raised mainly by his father and his grandparents, Mercer had received music lessons from his father and had also studied at music schools. By the time he had turned 20, he was leading his own band. Although he was a talented musician—particularly as a composer—he found it difficult to escape from comparisons with his famous father.

Mercer led his own groups off and on for more than 20 years, but with only limited success. His own music usually suffered when compared with his father's. At times, his father deliberately seemed to discourage Mercer from leading his own band. Duke Ellington was very competitive with other bandleaders throughout his career, and this was apparently true even with his own son.

Mercer grew to resent both his father's treatment and the expectations created by being his son. Finally, realizing that there was no way to escape from his dilemma if he wanted to have a musical career, he joined his father's band on a full-time basis, serving as the road manager and playing in the trumpet section. He did very well in both positions and contributed greatly to the survival and success of the Orchestra in the last decade of his father's life. ◖◗

Ellington celebrates his 65th birthday with companion Evie Ellis, who was a constant presence in his life for more than 35 years.

9

"DUKE'S PLACE"

T HE CIVIL RIGHTS movement in the 1960s brought great changes to the lives of all black Americans. No longer did the laws of the nation and the individual states work against the rights of black citizens. After much struggle and protest, they began to achieve equality with other Americans through years of nonviolent demonstrations and landmark legal cases.

Ellington followed these developments with great interest and approval, and he continued to compose works that celebrated the talents and accomplishments of the black race. However, he did not take an active leadership role in the civil rights movement and consequently received much criticism from black leaders. Because he was one of the best known and most successful blacks in America, many people believed that this gave him a responsibility to work actively to help his race. When he failed to do so, many blacks became disappointed in him.

But it was simply not Ellington's nature to take a large public role in the civil rights movement. A very private person, he preferred to make his own quiet contribution to the cause by writing music that was dedicated to his race. Throughout most of his life, it was difficult—if not dangerous—for a black person to speak out against racial discrimination in America. Even though this was no longer true in the

A talented composer and arranger, Mercer Ellington (shown looking over his father's shoulder) joined the Orchestra on a permanent basis in 1964, playing in the trumpet section and also serving as the band's road manager.

1960s, it was not realistic to expect Ellington, who was in his mid-sixties, to suddenly become an active spokesperson for black civil rights.

Instead, Ellington chose to show his support not through words and actions but through his music. He wrote an ambitious show called My People and dedicated it to the accomplishments of black Americans. The show, which played in Chicago in 1963, was very well received.

A major disappointment occurred for Ellington in 1965. He had been recommended by the nominating committee to receive the Pulitzer Prize, a tremendous honor given to the most accomplished individuals in journalism, literature, and music. Being nominated is usually a simple formality that precedes being given the award. However, in Ellington's case, the selection board made the unusual decision of ignoring the committee's recommendation. There were rumors of racial bias behind the selection board's decision, indicating that they felt a black jazz musician was not worthy of receiving such a prestigious award.

Ellington felt that he deserved the Pulitzer Prize, and he was deeply hurt by what happened. However, he tried to deal with the slight with characteristic good humor. "Fate is being very kind to me," the 66-year-old composer said. "Fate doesn't want me to be too famous, too young."

Ellington's disappointment soon disappeared as he became involved in other projects. In 1965, he was asked to give a concert to celebrate the opening of Grace Cathedral in San Francisco, California. This request prompted him to write the first of three sets of religious music that he called the Sacred Concerts. These concerts consisted of both vocal and instrumental music and were composed to be performed in large churches and cathedrals. The strong religious beliefs that his mother had passed on to him were helpful in writing the music.

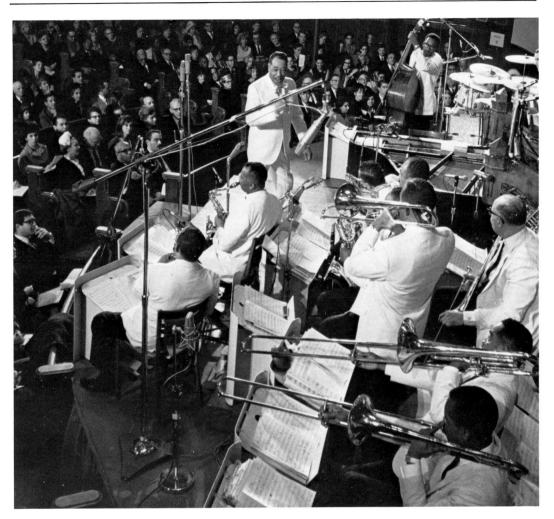

In the Sacred Concerts, Ellington tried to express his feelings and beliefs about God and about man's relationship with God. Although these concerts contained serious, reverent music, they also included elements of Ellington's jazz style and incorporated the musical personalities of his soloists. Accordingly, the Sacred Concerts were religious music that mixed joyousness with solemnity.

After introducing each Sacred Concert in an appropriately majestic church setting, Ellington performed them in many other places. The Sacred

Ellington conducts his Orchestra during a 1965 performance of his First Sacred Concert at the Fifth Avenue Presbyterian Church in New York City. His three Sacred Concerts were ambitious religious works that utilized the talents of singers and dancers along with various bandmembers.

Among the many honors that Ellington received were two Grammy Awards given to him in 1968 by the National Academy of Recording Arts and Sciences, the ruling body of the record industry. One was a special honorary award and the other was an award for Best Large Jazz Group.

Concerts were greeted with much enthusiasm by audiences, religious leaders, and music critics. Consequently, they helped to advance Ellington's reputation as a major composer.

In 1967, Billy Strayhorn died. Ellington was greatly saddened by the loss of his close friend and collaborator, who had assisted him in all of his triumphs over the past 29 years. Later in the year, Ellington recorded *And His Mother Called Him Bill*, an album of Strayhorn's compositions. The record was meant to serve as Ellington's loving tribute to his partner.

Strayhorn's death seemed to inspire Ellington to work at an even greater pace than usual. When not touring or recording, the Orchestra often played long engagements at the Rainbow Grill, a New York night spot. The band also made appearances at the Newport and Monterey jazz festivals. In 1968, the National Academy of Recording Arts and Sciences honored Ellington's achievements by giving him two Grammy Awards.

To celebrate his 70th birthday, Ellington was invited to the White House. After his first visit there in 1931, he and his Orchestra had been invited there to play before three presidents. However, this visit in 1969 was an altogether different occasion. He was honored at a formal dinner party, during which President Richard Nixon presented him with the Medal of Freedom, the highest award that the federal government can give to a civilian. After the awards ceremony, there was a concert in which an all-star jazz band entertained the guests with Ellington's music. Among those attending were his sister, Ruth; his son, Mercer; Mercer's wife and their three children; Count Basie; Benny Goodman; Willie "the Lion" Smith; and political leaders, musicians, writers, and other notable figures in American life.

Ellington could not resist the temptation to join in on the celebration and play the piano. It was a wonderful night for him. Honored by his country in the city of his birth, in the presidential mansion where his father had once worked as a waiter, he had clearly come a long way.

As Duke Ellington and His Orchestra entered the 1970s, age began to catch up with many of the musicians. Even those members who first joined the band in the 1950s had already been with the band for 15 years or more. Many were ready to retire, and they were replaced by younger musicians. Harry Carney and Paul Gonsalves remained, and Cootie Williams, the trumpet star of the 1930s, returned to the band. However, in 1970, Johnny Hodges, who had been an important part of the Ellington sound for so long, died suddenly of a heart attack.

During a celebration at the White House in honor of his 70th birthday, Ellington shares the piano with Willie "the Lion" Smith, an old friend from his early days in Harlem.

Even without such longtime companions as Stray-horn and Hodges, Ellington continued his activities without interruption. In 1970, he toured Europe, Australia, and the Orient. In 1971, he toured South America and made his first trip to the Soviet Union, where he discovered that he had enthusiastic fans behind the iron curtain. In 1972, the band made its longest visit ever to Asia. In 1973, they traveled to Africa and Europe, where they gave a Royal Command Performance for Queen Elizabeth of Great Britain.

Amid these travels, Ellington continued to receive frequent honors and awards for his many achievements. He had become recognized as a national treasure thanks to his unique musical genius. Although he was no longer producing popular hit songs like he had many decades before, he was still creating ambitious works that he felt would ensure his place in history as a major composer. *New Orleans Suite, Afro-Eurasian Eclipse,* and *The River* (a score written for a ballet) were some of the major compositions from this period.

Along with all of these activities, Ellington was also putting the finishing touches on his autobiography, *Music Is My Mistress.* After working on the book for several years, it finally appeared in 1973. It is exactly the kind of book one would expect a very private person such as Ellington to write about himself: It reveals very little about his feelings toward his music and his career.

Such a busy schedule may have proven to be demanding for Ellington's younger band members, but for him it had become a way of life. Mercer, serving as the band's road manager as well as his general assistant, was a great help to his father during these strenuous stretches of time. However, sometimes Ellington seemed to be showing his age. He occasionally appeared very tired. At other times, he acted irritably toward those around him. When he

did not seem to notice that the band was playing sloppily at some performances, it was an indication that he was not feeling well.

In early 1973, Ellington's doctor and best friend, Arthur Logan, discovered why he looked and felt so weak and tired: He was suffering from lung cancer, and the disease was spreading very quickly through his body. Ellington knew immediately that he had only a short time to live! Rather than relax and rest, or seek hospital treatment, he kept on working, never indicating that he was worried about his illness. The tours continued as scheduled, as did the flow of new compositions.

Shortly after Ellington completed his *Third Sacred Concert*, he premiered the work in October 1973 in London's historic Westminster Abbey. He did so despite the fact that he was feeling very weak. The concert, which was sponsored by the United Nations, was not a complete success. Yet it contained enough

Ellington gives a free concert in the streets of Harlem in 1970. Although he maintained a residence in the area from 1923 until his death, he was forced to spend long periods of time away from his home because of his band's many tours.

satisfying elements to please most of the listeners.

As Ellington's illness became worse, death seemed to be closing in all around him. Arthur Logan died in a mysterious accident and Evie, Ellington's long-time companion, was also diagnosed as suffering from lung cancer. Then, in January 1974, Ellington collapsed on stage during a performance. He could no longer ignore the effects of his illness, and he entered Presbyterian Hospital in New York.

Even while Ellington was still in the hospital, he felt the need to write music. Accordingly, he arranged for an electric piano to be placed in his hospital room. He resumed working on *Queenie Pie*, an opera that he had started several years before.

On April 29, 1974, a concert featuring Ellington's Orchestra was held to celebrate his 75th birthday.

Ten thousand people filled the Cathedral of St. John the Divine in New York City on May 27, 1974, for Ellington's funeral. Music from his Second Sacred Concert *was included in the service.*

Because he was far too ill to attend the concert, an associate had to direct the band, which performed selections from the Sacred Concerts. Ellington died less than a month later, on May 24. His funeral took place on May 27, at the Cathedral of St. John the Divine in Harlem. The funeral service featured music from the *Second Sacred Concert.* The 10,000 people who were in attendance also heard a number of public figures praise the great bandleader and composer, who was then buried in a New York cemetery next to his parents.

Mercer Ellington subsequently took over as the leader of the Duke Ellington Orchestra, and he has proven to be more than capable of meeting the challenge of following in his father's footsteps. Despite the death or retirement of each of the band members from the Orchestra's greatest years, Mercer has maintained a first-class band to perform his father's works. The Duke Ellington Orchestra continues to thrive today.

Ellington's music also lives on in other ways. Many pop singers, jazz groups, and dance orchestras continue to feature his songs in their performances. *Sophisticated Ladies*, a musical revue built around many of Ellington's numbers, opened in New York's theater district in 1981. Mercer served as musical director for the Broadway show, which was a big success and introduced a new generation of listeners to Ellington's music.

Having created a wealth of music that remains unmatched by any other jazz composer, Ellington knew how to make music that excites and entertains. Today, his majestic name still reigns over the jazz world as surely as it did a half century ago. Just as he was able to blend the various talents of his musicians into a finely crafted orchestra, so he managed to elevate a popular form of music into serious art. Such was the magic of Duke Ellington. ◖◗

Ellington's music returned to New York City in 1981 as the basis for a hit Broadway musical, Sophisticated Ladies.

APPENDIX

SELECTED DISCOGRAPHY

No words can adequately describe Duke Ellington's music. Anyone who has not had a chance to hear it should listen to at least one of his recordings. If it is not possible to purchase an Ellington album, one can usually be borrowed from a public or school library.

Over the course of Ellington's long career, he recorded for many different record companies, sometimes rerecording some of his earlier works. This can make it very confusing to know where to start when seeking out his music. The following albums offer a good introduction to Ellington's music. They are classic recordings and are all highly recommended.

Duke Ellington's Greatest Hits (Columbia Records). This album features excellent rerecordings of Ellington's most popular compositions.

Newport 1956 (Columbia Records). This recording of the Orchestra's great comeback concert at the Newport Jazz Festival includes Paul Gonsalves's exciting tenor sax solo on "Diminuendo and Crescendo in Blue."

The Blanton-Webster Band (RCA Records). This four-record set concentrates on the classic years from 1940 to 1942.

The Carnegie Hall Concerts: January 1943 (Prestige Records). This recording of Ellington's first concert at historic Carnegie Hall includes the only complete version of *Black, Brown, and Beige.*

The Ellington Era, Volume I (Columbia Records). This three-record set covers the period from 1927 to 1940 and is another fine example of Ellington's early work.

This Is Duke Ellington (RCA Records). This two-record set includes many of Ellington's greatest recordings from 1927 to 1945 and is probably the best place to start a collection of his music.

CHRONOLOGY

April 29, 1899	Born Edward Kennedy Ellington in Washington, D.C.
1917	Begins career as a professional pianist
1918	Starts to lead his own bands; marries Edna Thompson
1919	Son, Mercer, is born
1923	Ellington moves to New York City; first regular job with the Washingtonians
1925	Makes first live radio broadcast and first recordings
1926	Irving Mills becomes manager and business partner
Dec. 4, 1927	Ellington's band opens at the Cotton Club in Harlem
1928	Johnny Hodges joins the band
1930	"Mood Indigo" becomes Ellington's first hit
1931	The band leaves the Cotton Club and begins to tour the country
1933	First European tour
1935	Ellington's mother dies
1937	Ellington's father dies
1939	Second European tour; Billy Strayhorn joins the band
1940	Signs with Victor Recording Company
1941	"Take the A Train" becomes a hit; *Jump for Joy* is produced
1943	First Carnegie Hall concert
1951	Hodges, Sonny Greer, and Lawrence Brown leave the band
1955	Hodges returns to the band
1956	Ellington signs contract with Columbia Records; the band makes a comeback at the Newport Jazz Festival
1963	*My People* is produced
1965	Ellington gives the first Sacred Concert
1967	Strayhorn dies
1969	Ellington receives the Medal of Freedom
1970	Hodges dies
1973	*Music Is My Mistress* is published
May 24, 1974	Ellington dies in New York City

FURTHER READING

Anderson, Jervis. *This Was Harlem 1900–1950*. New York: Farrar, Straus & Giroux, 1981.

Collier, James Lincoln. *Duke Ellington*. New York: Oxford University Press, 1987.

Dance, Stanley. *The World of Duke Ellington*. New York: Scribners, 1970.

Ellington, Duke. *Music Is My Mistress*. New York: Doubleday, 1973.

Ellington, Mercer. *Duke Ellington in Person*. Boston: Houghton Mifflin, 1978.

George, Don. *Sweet Man*. New York: Putnam, 1981.

Haskins, Jim. *The Cotton Club*. New York: New American Library, 1977.

Jewell, Derek. *Duke*. New York: Norton, 1977.

Lambert, G. E. *Duke Ellington*. Cranbury, NJ: Barnes, 1959.

Sales, Grover. *Jazz: America's Classical Music*. Englewood Cliffs, NJ: Prentice-Hall, 1984.

Tirro, Frank. *Jazz: A History*. New York: Norton, 1977.

Williams, Martin. *The Jazz Tradition*. New York: Oxford University Press, 1983.

INDEX